REGULATORY REFORM

HIGHLIGHTS OF A
CONFERENCE ON GOVERNMENT REGULATION

held in Washington, D.C.
on 10-11 September 1975

Edited by W. S. Moore

American Enterprise Institute
for Public Policy Research
1150 17th Street, N.W., Washington, D. C. 20036

Domestic Affairs Study 45, March 1976
Price $2.00 per copy

© Copyright 1976 by the American Enterprise Institute
for Public Policy Research, Washington, D. C.
Permission to quote from or to reproduce materials in
this publication is granted when due acknowledgment is made.

Library of Congress Catalog Card No. 76–5253
ISBN 0–8447–3208–7

PARTICIPANTS

Stuart Altman
Deputy Assistant Secretary for Health Planning and Analysis
Department of Health, Education and Welfare

Clarence Brown
U.S. Representative (Republican, Ohio)

Rita Ricardo Campbell
Senior Fellow, The Hoover Institution on War, Revolution and Peace

Philip Caper, M.D.
Staff, Senate Subcommittee on Health

Paul Cunningham
Staff Counsel, Senate Subcommittee on Surface Transportation

Carl Curtis
U.S. Senator (Republican, Nebraska)

Charles DiBona
Executive Vice President, American Petroleum Institute

John Dingell
U.S. Representative (Democrat, Michigan)

John Erlenborn
U.S. Representative (Republican, Illinois)

H. E. Frech III
Assistant Professor of Economics
University of California at Santa Barbara

Ann Friedlaender
Professor of Economics and Civil Engineering
Massachusetts Institute of Technology

Paul Ginsburg
Assistant Professor, Departments of Economics and Community Medicine
Michigan State University

Mark Green
Director, Corporate Accountability Research Group

Robert Helms
Director, Health Policy Studies
American Enterprise Institute for Public Policy Research

Hendrik Houthakker
Professor of Economics, Harvard University

Hubert Humphrey
U.S. Senator (Democrat, Minnesota)

George W. James
Senior Vice President, Air Transport Association of America

Paul MacAvoy
Member, Council of Economic Advisers

James C. Miller III
Senior Staff Economist, Council of Economic Advisers

Thomas Gale Moore
Senior Fellow, The Hoover Institution on War, Revolution and Peace

Ralph Nader
Founder, Center for Study of Responsive Law
and numerous other consumer/public interest organizations

Joseph Newhouse
Senior Staff Economist, Rand Corporation

Roger Noll
Professor of Economics, California Institute of Technology

G. Warren Nutter
Paul Goodloe McIntire Professor of Economics
University of Virginia

A. Daniel O'Neal
Vice Chairman, Interstate Commerce Commission

Ronald Reagan
Former Governor of California

Benjamin Rosenthal
U.S. Representative (Democrat, New York)

Antonin Scalia
Assistant Attorney General
Office of Legal Counsel, U.S. Department of Justice

Gary Seevers
Commissioner, Commodity Futures Trading Commission

Eileen Shanahan
Reporter, *New York Times* Washington Bureau

John Snow
Deputy Under Secretary, U.S. Department of Transportation

Robert Spann
Assistant Professor of Economics
Virginia Polytechnic Institute and State University

William Springer
Commissioner, Federal Power Commission

Lee White
Former Chairman, Federal Power Commission

Ralph K. Winter, Jr.
Professor of Law, Yale Law School

CONTENTS

INTRODUCTION

This booklet presents a brief edited version of the highlights of the Conference on Regulatory Reform, held in Washington, D. C., on 10–11 September 1975, under the joint sponsorship of the American Enterprise Institute and the Hoover Institution. The full conference proceedings will also be published, while the televised panel discussion that occurred on the evening of 11 September is already available from AEI on audio and video cassettes and in pamphlet form. The format of this booklet closely follows the chronology of the conference.

To present only the highlights from this conference has involved drastic editing of the papers, formal presentations, and discussions. Rather than attempting to summarize the entire proceedings, the editor has chosen to present, as far as possible, excerpts selected both for their general interest and as representative of the variety of opinions expressed by the participants. Omissions are not indicated. The reader will find the full text of the conference papers in the forthcoming proceedings volume. The editor trusts that the highlights presented here will serve to introduce the major issues raised during the conference.

While issues of regulatory reform have arisen many times since creation of the first regulatory agency, the current administration in particular has cited reexamination of the regulatory system as an item high on its priority list. It is the purpose of conferences such as this to assist in that reexamination by bringing together members of the administration and Congress, lawyers, academicians, and representatives from industry and the public to present their views.

POWER-ENERGY REGULATION

Professor Robert Spann opened the power-energy regulation session of the conference by advocating increased flexibility in the application of existing electric utility regulation. Charles DiBona discussed the specific problems of regulation of the petroleum industry. He concluded that the industry is so burdened by government regulation that it is now in a phase of "regulatory overkill."

ROBERT SPANN

Federal Regulation of Electric Utilities Via Taxation and Litigation

No one is happy with the results of electric utility regulation today. Consumers are upset about the price of electricity. While electric utility prices are increasing at a rapid rate, the profitability of electric utilities is declining at a relatively rapid rate, although that trend has reversed somewhat in the past few months. The traditional textbook model of the state regulatory agency and the process of public utility regulation as a means of solving the "problem of natural monopoly" is being subjected to increasing criticism. In many instances, state regulatory commissions have been criticized for failing to grant "adequate" rate increases. In others, it has been argued that regulatory commissions and regulated utilities utilize inefficient pricing systems. Current regulatory practices that relate prices to previously observed accounting costs and which lead to substantial adjudication delays have come under increasing attack. Various forms of automatic adjustment mechanisms (such as fuel adjustment clauses which automatically adjust rates as fuel prices change) have come under increasing attack from a wide variety of sources.

A basic problem with current regulatory practices, including the pricing of the output of regulated electric utilities, is their inflexibility in the face of rapidly changing conditions. The traditional approach of utility regulation was designed during periods of relative price stability. One should therefore not be surprised to find that during periods of instability in both the level of absolute and relative prices, regulatory institutions come under increasing attack. Thus, a key element of any policy of regulatory reform within the existing institutional framework should be the inclusion of policies which increase the flexibility of regulatory institutions.

Recently we have seen that in periods of high rates of inflation utility profitability falls dramatically. This is in contrast to periods of low rates of inflation, such as the early 1960s, in which utilities were earning relatively high rates of return, and investments in utilities, in many cases in the early 1960s, were more profitable than investments in industrial firms. One reason for this may simply be that the regulatory process is lengthy and has lags involved in it.

Prices for, say 1976, are quite often set on the basis of 1974 or 1975 costs. Conversely, prices in the early 1960s, when firms had gone as many as ten years without general rate cases, were set on the basis of costs that were observed, say, in the early 1950s, which were somewhat higher than those present in the 1960s. If costs are falling over time and there is a considerable lag between the time costs change and regulators act, firms make money considerably above any normal or competitive rate of return. When costs are rising over time, prices are kept below cost and firms lose money. If one takes 1973 utility assets of $108 billion and goes through some calculations, he finds that just changing from a rate of inflation of 5 percent to 8 percent imposes losses on utilities roughly of the magnitude of $1 billion to $3.4 billion per year—for an industry in which 1973 revenues were approximately $26 billion and 1974 revenues were almost $40 billion.

Electricity is largely a non-storable resource. Capacity is built to meet a maximum rate of demand. Electric utilities have an array of plants with different variable costs. Lower variable cost plants are utilized most intensely while higher variable cost plants are utilized more intensely during peak periods and less intensely at other times. The optimum pricing scheme in such a situation is a system of peak-load pricing, in which a much higher price is charged during periods of peak consumption, and lower prices during the off-peak period. For most utilities in the East, this peak period would be summer periods from around noon to 9:00 p.m.

Historically, we have not seen such pricing policies pursued by utilities. The pricing policies we have seen pursued are policies of declining block rates. Even in cases where utilities have loose forms of peak-load pricing in the case of commercial industrial tariffs, the peak charge or capacity charge is generally extremely low relative to long-run marginal cost of providing capacity.

I assume for purposes of illustration a very simple model of the electric utility and, in fact, take into account only the cost of producing electricity. I do not include the cost of transmitting electricity via transmission system or distributing electricity within a neighborhood—for the most part just the cost of plant. Even with such a simple model, and even if we use some very low elasticities of demand for electricity, the effects of pricing reforms in regulation can be quite large. The estimated change in the average price of electricity from instituting more efficient pricing would be a reduction of between 3.6 percent and 38 percent. The reason one would observe such a fall in the average price of electricity is that if one priced peak capacity higher, this would lead to lower capacity requirements and thus lower overall average cost to the system.

There is some evidence, and intuition tends to confirm it, that the elasticity of demand for electricity is somewhat higher during off-peak periods than during peak periods. For example, in the case of an eastern utility with a high summer peak during the daytime hours, the demand for electricity at that time period might be less elastic than the demand for electricity during off-peak hours. If that is the case and if prices rise uniformly in all time periods, people will tend to cut their consumption back most during the off-peak period. We have seen utility load factors decline in the last year. Some utilities, within the last four years, have had load-factor declines in excess of 10 percent; in other words, their capacity utilization has fallen by more than 10 percent. If this happens, one would expect the utility to lose money. If the utility is charging the same prices in all time periods and costs go up, prices go up and capacity utilization falls.

Look at two rather simple examples: One, a 100 percent increase in fuel costs, which is about what was observed during 1974; and, two, a 24 percent increase in capital costs. Even if those costs are instantaneously included in rates—no effects of regulatory lag—a 100 percent increase in fuel costs can impose losses on utilities (even with low elasticities of demand) ranging from $260 million to $1.89 billion. An approximately 24 percent increase in capital costs can impose losses on utilities ranging from $100 million to $1.2 billion. Those are fairly large numbers. The losses are due mainly to a change in the composition of output because different outputs have different marginal costs, but are all charged the same.

The problem with fuel adjustment clauses, by themselves, is that while they do provide a relatively cheap method of regulation, they apply to one input only, and one can obviously see that if the firm is automatically allowed to pass on fuel cost increases but not allowed to pass on capital cost increases, it pays the firm to be more fuel-intensive than it would be otherwise.

There are policies that can be pursued that would tend to increase the efficiency of regulated markets. The short-term alternatives that appear to be the most efficient method of improving regulatory performance are increased use of more efficient pricing schemes such as peak-load pricing and increased usage of adjustment clauses that automatically adjust rates as input prices change. Such policies would increase the flexibility and efficiency of regulation and allow regulatory policy to respond more rapidly than at present to changes in factor prices and other exogenous factors. While these policy recommendations would tend to improve the efficiency and flexibility of regulated markets, they are at best short-term solutions to what may really be a long-term problem.

Regulatory policies operate as simple pricing rules or constraints on the behavior of firms and induce subtle distortions in input usage and pricing policies. They are an attempt to duplicate the workings of the market mechanism. One should not and cannot expect simple constraints on firm behavior to lead to results which replicate the workings of the free market. Peak-load pricing, for example, involves increased metering equipment. Automatic adjustment clauses are essentially a form of mark-up pricing and do not always duplicate the price adjustments that might be observed in a competitive market. Thus, the benefits to existing institutions, while positive, could be less than expected.

The result of examining in detail policies which improve the efficiency of regulated markets within existing institutions is that while such policies can be located, and while they might have substantial benefits, the examination tends to strengthen the argument for a more serious consideration of the adoption of selective policies of deregulating certain segments of the electric utility industry.

4

CHARLES DiBONA

Regulatory Overkill

The petroleum industry is probably one of the most heavily regulated industries in the nation today. Government can largely dictate to oil people where they can look for oil, where they can locate pipelines, where they can put refineries, what they can make in the way of products, to whom they can sell the products, where, in what quantities, and at what price. This pattern of regulation, I believe, has greatly reduced the efficiency and the effectiveness of the petroleum industry. This is not to suggest that the people in our industry think that all regulation is bad or that we advocate a return to a laissez-faire economic system. But we feel that regulation of the petroleum industry has simply gone too far and is now in the phase of "regulatory overkill."

During the 1973–74 oil embargo the supply of crude available to various refineries in the nation differed substantially. In a well-intentioned effort to spread out the shortage the Federal Energy Office established an allocation program requiring those refineries with relatively large supplies of crude to sell some of their supply to those refineries relatively short of crude. The maximum price the selling refiner could charge for crude sold under this program was the weighted average price of its total crude supply. The idea was to even out both supplies and costs of crude oil among refineries during the embargo. However, in their concern to manage the shortage, the regulators forgot that the way to solve the shortage was to get a larger total supply of crude.

Under the allocation program, there were powerful incentives for individual refiners to cut down their purchase of imported oil, thereby reducing the total supply of crude available to consumers. Foreign oil was selling, on average, at prices substantially above domestic price-controlled oil. Thus, refiners with relatively little domestic crude had an incentive to reduce their imports and buy oil through the allocation program at a price less than the import price. Refiners with large supplies of domestic oil, on the other hand, found themselves forced to sell oil at a weighted-average acquisition cost which was less than the cost of the last barrel they bought from foreign sources. Thus, refiners with relatively large supplies of crude were also encouraged to cut back their imports of foreign oil. Thus, the allocation program actually discouraged foreign oil imports during the embargo. This was opposed to the national interest.

Under the authority granted in the Emergency Petroleum Allocation Act, the FEA has maintained a two-tier price system for crude oil in the United States. As you have been hearing so often lately, "old" oil, from properties in production before 1972, was price-controlled at $5.25 per barrel. Imported oil, "new" domestic oil, stripper-well oil and "released" oil are exchanged at world market prices. Because refineries have varying access to these sources of oil, the cost of crude to different refiners varies markedly. To offset these differences, the "entitlements" program was started. This program makes the supply of price-controlled domestic crude oil available proportionately to all refiners. This practice results in refiners with relatively large supplies of "old" crude oil making payments to refiners with relatively small supplies of "old" crude oil.

5

Most supporters of these price controls believe that this policy prevents OPEC from setting domestic oil prices and weakens the cartel. However, analysis shows that price controls and entitlements actually work to strengthen the OPEC cartel in both the short and long run. By holding the domestic price of "old" oil and thus the average price of all oil consumed under the world market price, the United States is encouraging consumption in both the short and longer run, and price control on old oil is discouraging the longer run supply expansion from "old" oil fields.

Ironically, the "old" oil price ceiling provides a subsidy to OPEC oil importers. Because of the "entitlements program" that accompanies the price ceiling, those refiners importing oil at the market price are given a share in the pool of price-controlled oil. This practice subsidizes the importation of every barrel of foreign oil and increases the total imports into the United States. Here we see a program designed first to control prices and later to even out costs to refiners. While the two-tier pricing and entitlements program may generally achieve those objectives, the longer run objectives of energy policy are being thwarted. The price controls and the entitlements program are encouraging domestic consumption, subsidizing the importation of foreign oil, and discouraging domestic supply expansion of "old" oil properties.

The longer history of price regulation of natural gas provides an example of what could happen to the oil business under continuing counterproductive regulation. Natural gas producers have been subject to interstate price regulation since 1954. Rate regulation prevented prices from rising in response to growing demand, thereby reducing the incentive to expand supply at the same time that the lower prices encouraged consumption. The effort to hold prices below a market clearing level has created a shortage which imposes great costs to the economy. What is ironic about the natural gas situation is that rather than freeing the market price to allocate the existing gas supply and encourage new supply development, some observers would expand controls to intrastate markets and allocate supplies to consumers.

Markets are very efficient at matching up buyers and sellers through a process of constant adjustment. Attempts to regulate markets typically use some historical base period, freeze a set of conditions as of that base period, and then provide a mechanism to consider special cases. This is the procedure that was used during the oil embargo. Gasoline supplies were allocated to regions according to the supplies received in 1972. Essentially each wholesaler was to supply the same quantity to the same retail dealers as in the 1972 base period. The system did not work well for the simple reason that it was based on a static concept while the world was changing. Population growth rates change, weather patterns change, tastes change, and marketing patterns are altered. As a result, during the embargo, some areas had no gasoline lines at service stations while other areas had horrendous lines. One cannot help suggesting that the price system could have done a much better job of allocating supplies and eliminating long lines at gasoline stations than any system based on historical precedent.

There are three persistent ideas that are advanced in support of continued economic controls on the U.S. oil industry, all of which are wrong. First is the idea that there must be a double standard in every regulation that says in effect, "We must make it tough on the big guys and help the little guys." This idea is illustrated by a bill now before the Senate which provides different selling prices for three kinds of producers of natural gas. "Small producers" may sell at a price 50 percent over the controlled price; so-called "independent producers"—companies with less than a billion dollars of assets—can sell at a price equal to the new domestic price for crude oil on a BTU basis; and finally just plain "producers" will sell at a fixed price prescribed by the FPC under a cost methodology spelled out by Congress. This proposal is clearly nonproductive in our economy. There should be a single standard for all who compete.

The second idea is that there is no competition in the oil industry and that controls are needed to offset what is called "the monopoly power of large oil companies." About the only evidence ever offered in support of this bafflingly incorrect contention is that several U.S. oil companies are among the largest corporations in the country. I would simply point out that size and monopoly power are not necessarily synonymous. In petroleum there are many large and small firms competing for business. Available research suggests that there is no basis for government intervention because of monopoly power. The competitive nature of the petroleum industry is clear when three factors are examined: first, the lack of concentration; second, the freedom of entry for new competitors; and, third, the history of modest rates of return.

There are more than 10,000 producers of crude oil, 131 refining companies, and over 15,000 wholesalers of petroleum products competing for business. No firm controls more than 11 percent of the national volume at any of the levels of industry operation. In fact, the petroleum industry is less concentrated than the average for all U.S. industries and considerably less concentrated than most other important industries. There are no barriers to prevent the entry of firms that might want to begin to operate in the petroleum business. The use of joint ventures in both bidding for leases and in production has served to lower entry barriers to crude oil and natural gas production. Thus, not only is there active competition from existing firms but also the frequent injection of additional competition from new firms.

The profits of the industry—when compared with those of other industries—have been moderate on average, another sign of competition. Over the ten-year period from 1965 through 1974, the average return on stockholder equity for the petroleum industry was 13.4 percent, slightly more than the average return for all U.S. manufacturing (13 percent) but less than the return on mining (14.7 percent). The 1974 profits produced a 19.9 percent return, but the unusual quality of that year is shown by a comparison of the first half of 1974 which produced a 20.1 percent average rate of return with the first half of 1975 when the average rate of return was 11.9 percent. A more instructive measure of petroleum industry profitability is return on total assets. In the first six months of 1975 this stood at 6.1 percent, down from 11.1 percent in the same period of 1974. It seems unreasonable to continue controls or to pass legislation changing the structure of the industry where a viable competitive structure already is operating.

The third erroneous idea assumes that prices to consumers in a competitive industry can in the long run be reduced through controls. The consumer pays the increased costs that would occur anyway under a market price system, but he must pay two other costs. First, he must pay the cost of inefficiencies that would be eliminated under market price competition but which thrive under price controls, and second, he must pay the cost of supporting the huge bureaucracy and the huge special information systems necessary to run the controls. I question how many consumers, given full information about the consequences of oil price controls, would opt for their continuation.

Commentaries

LEE WHITE: In about two weeks, eleven people will assemble in Vienna and decide our market prices. That is what we are asked to accept as the free market. Now, I can remember when the petroleum industry believed that regulation was not all bad: I remember that we had an oil import quota program from 1959 to 1973. The program said, in effect, that the world price of oil was too low and that we needed to keep that low-priced oil out and protect the domestic industry in order to produce domestic oil so that we would not have to be dependent upon unstable governments elsewhere in the world. That was a form of regulation that cost the American consumer—these are tricky figures— roughly $7 billion a year or about $85 billion all told. Maybe it was worth it, but it was regulation.

I come with my package of prejudices and biases and I believe that regulation is not necessarily a desirable way to go. It just happens to be the best of all the bad alternatives: after debate, I find myself believing that regulation is what is required to serve the public interest. Mr. DiBona suggested that the industry really is competitive. I wonder how four United States senators can say in a public letter to the industry, "For heaven's sake, can't you fellows keep the price down a little bit for a while?" If the industry is competitive, how in the world can you expect the president of a petroleum company to say, "You know, the price really could go higher, but I hope the stockholders won't mind if I give this one to the public." It just blows your mind.

WILLIAM SPRINGER: Some two years ago our commission suggested deregulation of new natural gas. There was a strong feeling at the commission that we could not deregulate all gas immediately. In the first place, we could not get full deregulation through the Congress, which is a pretty good reason for not bringing it up. The second reason was that we thought it would have a tremendous inflationary effect upon the economy. We thought that if all gas were deregulated at one time, there would be an astronomical jump in price which would be reflected ripple-wise in the whole economy. As our staff worked it out, by deregulating new gas it would take ten to fifteen years to deregulate the entire industry. This was one thing we thought would be successful.

With gas at fifty-two cents, which is the national rate, with $1.00 for coal on an equivalent BTU basis, and $1.50 or maybe $2.00 for oil, the question arises: can we continue to have one of the three big sources of energy at one-third or one-half the price of the others? The ill effects of this price disparity are one important reason why there should be a gradual change until these energy sources ultimately can become competitive, but that change will require action by the Congress, not just by the Federal Power Commission.

JOHN DINGELL: The regulatory process is like God or trade unions: if we did not have it, we would have to invent it. I suspect that the sooner we recognize the fact that government regulation is here to stay and probably will grow, the better off we will be in addressing the real problems that exist with regard to it. Good regulatory process given fair statutory backing will produce good and sensible regulation that will work and not exceed the bounds of need.

The budgets of regulatory bodies inside the federal structure are too small; the regulatory bodies have too few experts. There is interference from the administration in the regulatory process, in the substantive law and in appointments. Scandals are not infrequent inside these agencies. Recommendations for statutory change are carefully filtered by the administration. Agency requests for an adequate budget are usually summarily denied. The functioning of these agencies tends to be thwarted by the executive branch which tends to regard them as an arm of the executive, in clear defiance of both history and statute. The federal regulatory structure is entirely under the appointments power of the President. Personnel in federal regulatory agencies tend to flow back and forth between government and industry with very little input from outsiders. The most competent personnel frequently return to industry by reason of the inadequate pay structure inside these agencies.

Cases take far too long. The ICC still tinkers with the freight car shortage which was the first matter presented when the commission was set up in the 1880s. The Federal Communications Commission has the clear channel case, dating from the 1930s. The hard fact of the matter is that the Administrative Procedures Act, the due process clause and the structure of these agencies set up a situation where obfuscation and delay are the order of the day. For years the regulated industries have been making use of this situation and finding it delightful. The environmentalists have now begun to make use of it, and that has subjected them to intense criticism. What we really need is a major revamping of the process.

Many will tell you that the regulatory process has not worked and that we have to get rid of it because a free economy cannot co-exist with the regulatory process. I happen to agree that we should deregulate if we can ever get ourselves a free economy. In point of fact, there is not a free economy in any segment of the American society. In order to protect the American people, a strong and vigorous regulatory process is necessary in Washington.

CLARENCE BROWN: If regulatory reform is the answer, what is the question? I think the question is how to restore flexibility and credibility in government. Regulatory reform means that we should get the government out of activities that it cannot do or cannot do well. At the least, we should reduce the expectations for regulation. In recent years the federal government has been building high expectations for itself among its constituents and then failing to meet those expectations.

In his paper Professor Spann has properly identified "galloping inflation" as one of the causes of the breakdown of government ability to regulate the free enterprise system. When the rules keep changing rapidly or the economic results keep changing rapidly, it is very difficult to catch up in a regulatory system that has a lot of due process in it. And, of course, government regulation is not limited to rates, routes, and returns. It includes such government prerogatives as taking from one segment of society and giving to another. The use of eminent domain, licensing, zoning, and taxation are all part of the regulatory process whether we are willing to admit it or not.

Government itself frequently changes the rules by which regulators in another part of government have to make their judgments. Pollution control is not a major consideration set forth in the charters of most state utility commissions, but it certainly has an impact on the judgments they must make. We now have many regulatory agencies each of which deals with some portion of the economic and social problems that the regulated industry has to face. When one regulatory agency begins to make rapid changes—never mind the economic changes that occur with inflation—changes such as have been made by the Environmental Protection Agency with respect to the utility industry, then the other regulators must catch up or the industry will be caught in the crossfire of multiple regulation.

The free-market system is different. The newspaper business in which I have operated is one of the least regulated businesses, thanks to the First Amendment. When paper prices go up fast, then we either raise our ad rates or hold our wages down or increase our subscription rate or something else. Business may not be good for the retailers, so we may not be able to raise our advertising rates rapidly, but there is usually something we can do to offset the change. In regulated business the manager has less flexibility, and that means there must be more flexibility on the part of the regulators.

Regulation will always be with us. In some areas we can do better with regulation, but in others we ought to eliminate it. When I have doubts, I go to the folks back home. I believe that the people are telling me that they want me to stop doing so much *for* them because it does entirely too much *to* them.

MR. WHITE: As far as the natural gas industry is concerned, I cannot really condemn a management that says, "Listen, we are not going to stick our money into looking for natural gas in the United States as long as we have the option to go to the Sahara, the North Sea and the coast of Ecuador. That U.S. gas is going to stay there. It takes a lot of money to get that gas. We will get it, but not before Congress deregulates the price."

It is incumbent upon the Congress to reach a decision. My assessment is that the primary explanation for the natural gas shortage is that the industry is waiting for the Congress to tell it what the ground rules are. It is almost unconscionable for the Congress to have diddled around for three years on this subject without having decided anything.

CONGRESSMAN DINGELL: I am not one who thinks we have to rush out and pass a piece of legislation deregulating natural gas. We do have a natural gas crisis on our hands. What really is needed is for the Federal Power Commission to buckle down and regulate. I think that the FPC has authority to fix prices within those areas necessary to assure a reasonable supply in the market. There is an honest difference here on whether we have a free competitive economy. I assume that with natural gas, when a fellow has one supplier who delivers gas to his house, he does not have much choice and he is not the beneficiary of a free economy.

MR. WHITE: There is a recent California Public Utilities Commission decision that should be looked at. In the case, ARCO, which is going to do some drilling up in Prudhoe Bay for natural gas, told the southern gas companies that it would be willing to give the customers of those companies the first option to negotiate with Arco for the purchase of the gas provided the companies put up $320 million for the carrying charges. The commission said, "This is blackmail." On page 28 of that decision, the commission said, "A number of us were opposed to continued regulation of new gas. On the basis of what we have seen can be done by four companies in one producing area, we hereby publicly recant and recommend that natural gas regulation be continued."

MR. DiBONA: Lee White has questioned the view that artificially low prices are the cause of the natural gas shortage and attributes the shortage to the existence of potential investments overseas with higher rates of return. There are about 3,000 natural gas producers in the United States. I think most economists would agree that, if there were a reasonable rate of return commensurate with the risk here in the United States, potential overseas investments could not possibly have caused the shortage of natural gas in this country.

I want to talk briefly about the implications of prices being held below those set by the OPEC cartel. Holding prices below OPEC prices means that there will be some oil not produced in the United States that could be produced for less than it could be bought from the cartel. Let us say the cartel price is $11.00 a barrel. If there is oil in the United States that could be produced at $10.00 a barrel but is not produced because we hold the price below $10.00 and buy from the cartel instead, then this country as a whole is $1.00 poorer for each OPEC barrel we buy. This phenomenon will exist independently of the price the cartel sets. This analysis ignores the problem of wealth redistribution in the United States, taxation and a number of other matters, but the choice not to price oil in the United States at the free-market level makes us poorer.

LUNCHEON ADDRESS

At lunch, Dr. Paul MacAvoy discussed the various proposals for regulatory reform being considered by the Ford administration.

PAUL MACAVOY

Regulatory Reform: How To Get There from Here

For decades economists have been decrying the effects of economic regulation on the efficiency of the market economy. Countless articles, numerous commissions and many conferences have analyzed, criticized and recommended fundamental changes in regulation. As far as public policy has been concerned, however, this activity has produced no significant change. Yet now we find ourselves in a situation in which decidedly procompetitive regulatory reform legislation has been enacted for the securities industry and has been introduced or will be introduced shortly to reform such traditional targets as the Interstate Commerce Commission, the Civil Aeronautics Board, the Federal Power Commission and the fair trade laws.

Recently, several events and conditions have done more than economic research to heighten public interest in regulatory reform. The inflation since the late 1960s has prompted serious political concern with the causes and cures of inflation. It is not at all apparent that microeconomic regulation is a major cause of inflation, but a heightened awareness of prices has produced a suspicion of the regulatory mechanisms by which prices are determined.

Although deregulation policies have long been associated with classical economics, a more widespread understanding of the costs of regulation has made regulatory reform an increasingly nonpartisan issue. The nonpartisan flavor of the movement has probably also been helped by the increased participation of some consumer groups. The organized consumer does give politicians of all parties incentives at least to analyze the anticompetitive and proindustry aspects of regulatory agencies.

Most important, the prospects for regulatory reform have been improved by the sheer force of the market breakdown in certain regulated industries. Drastic reductions in the quality and quantity of rail service, substantial shortages of natural gas, and impending shortages of electric power capacity have been widely attributed to regulation. It is significant that governors from fourteen states facing natural gas shortages were recently able to accept deregulation of gas prices as a viable long-term solution even though the President specifically pointed out that prices will rise. This acceptance reflects an increasingly sophisticated awareness that lower regulated prices, with no product available, are not a preferred solution to any problem.

12

There are three basic approaches to regulatory reform. First, there is deregulation accomplished through repeal of basic legislation. Second, there is legislative reform of existing regulatory agencies and practices. Third, there is reform through administrative and procedural change within the regulatory agencies themselves, without legislative directive.

The economic arguments for total deregulation are appealing, particularly in natural gas and transportation. Immediate deregulation has not, however, been able to muster enough political support to be reflected in new legislation. There are several reasons for this. First, those who benefit from current regulatory policies have been able to obstruct deregulation through compromise in the Congress or elsewhere. Second, in a world where people are risk averse and lack perfect foresight, it is not unreasonable that the body politic should decide to proceed down the road to regulatory reform with caution. Third, the total deregulation approach seems to have been doomed in bureaucratic decision making because it lacks that room for compromise on which the stability of that process depends.

If total and abrupt deregulation appears to be too difficult politically, administrative change in practices, policies and personnel appears too easy to be an adequate solution. There is a view that the purposes of regulation are proper but that the result has turned out poorly primarily because of administrative difficulties. Numerous studies have called for organizational reforms to improve regulation, and have argued that the quality of regulation could be significantly improved if only regulatory agencies were not so independent, if only they were consolidated, if only they were staffed by better people, and so on.

Improved regulation can take two forms. First, we can upgrade the efficiency of the regulatory decision-making process. Second, we can improve the economic result of the decisions. Attention should be directed to both, but for lasting effects it should be focused on the economic result of the decisions. The administrative approach to regulatory reform overlooks a basic constraint: many agencies were created by and continue to operate under misdirected or misguided legislation. Regulatory practices can be improved over the long run only by legislative changes.

Suggestions that regulatory agencies should be either more dependent or more independent of Congress or the executive branch have been made many times. However, no matter where formal accountability rests, it seems that regulation remains a mechanism with potential for granting some individuals or groups economic gain at the expense of others. A move toward changing the direction of accountability from the Congress and the executive branch to true independence would tend to change the identity of lobbyists and lawyers without any clear prospect for an improvement in the economic effects from regulation.

Regulatory reform through internal changes should not be passed up. Indeed, recent developments in this area have been encouraging. The increased use of inflation impact statements and requirements for more benefit-cost analysis of regulatory actions have the potential for raising the quality of regulatory decision making. I am also hopeful that independent commissions will respond positively to requests that regulatory delays be reduced, competition be encouraged, and consumers be heard. The basic problem, however, is with the long-run results. Right now, while the regulatory reform movement has some momentum, the agencies are moving in directions that most observers would agree are desirable. But some years ahead, when the deregulators have spent themslves, it seems likely that agency policies will then reflect business as usual. Real and lasting reform requires legislative change in the legal powers and responsibilities of the regulatory agencies.

Much of the regulatory reform effort within the administration is aimed at statutory modifications of existing regulatory agencies. This approach is able to accommodate some compromises that are part of the political process. Over the past months, a relatively consistent pattern in the approach to regulatory reform has emerged. This pattern is evidenced in the types of specific reform measures being proposed in administration-sponsored legislation: increased pricing flexibility, liberalized entry regulation, and elimination of antitrust immunity. The consistency is also reflected in the manner in which these reforms will be implemented: through a phasing of deregulation.

The two most important types of provisions, from an economic point of view, have to do with pricing and entry. In transportation, the lack of pricing flexibility has inhibited the ability of sellers of services to meet the competition of substitute services. In other industries, the lack of price flexibility in the presence of severe inflation has put regulated companies out of the market so as to create shortages.

The administration proposes to provide regulated industries with increased pricing flexibility. This flexibility would create a zone of reasonableness—an expanding band within which regulated firms would be able to adjust their prices without agency interference. These bands are defined as percentage deviations up or down from published rate levels, allowing a float in the regulated price structure. In some cases, such as the setting of railroad rates, it has been proposed that the band be allowed to widen gradually over time, thus providing more effective competition in the long run. The financial institutions bill also reflects this approach of phased pricing flexibility in the provisions which free up the rate which may be paid on time deposits. In other legislation, such as in the forthcoming air transportation reform, we propose a zone based on prevention of both monopoly and predatory pricing.

As a second type of reform measure, the administration proposes the gradual liberalization of entry controls as the method by which increased pricing flexibility can be policed. In the proposed air transportation reforms, for example, only minimum constraints on entry would be in effect after a period of five years of progressive liberalization of certificate restrictions. Provisions to expedite agency processing of entry requests are also an important part of our reform proposals. These provisions move towards the goal of increasing competition through actual and potential entry, while minimizing the transitional adjustment costs of regulatory reform.

A third category of reform is the removal of antitrust immunity now granted to numerous industries. Such immunity serves to constrain competition by permitting industries to fix prices, pool revenues, and set capacity levels.

14

The administration's proposed transportation reform legislation specifically out-laws the anticompetitive activities of industry rate bureaus.

Throughout the administration's reform program, we have adopted a policy of gradual implementation of the reform measures. A scheduled program of phased regulatory change serves to minimize the potential for disruption and allows industry to plan ahead and adjust rationally to the change. And if it is asked why we are pursuing regulatory reform at all, the cynical answer is that there may be votes in it. But I think the correct answer is that the administration, new as it is, has already established economic efficiency as a basic policy objective. There is the recognition that the considerable costs of regulation have been borne for too long.

Discussion

STEVE MOTT, *Washington Post:* The airlines claim that deregulation is going to cause them to lose more money than they are losing right now. How do you propose to cut fares and yet inspire competition and have a better situation for consumers?

DR. MACAVOY: The approach we have taken is to try to obtain a good grasp on what the industry is going to be like over a five-to-ten-year period. If we look ahead five to ten years, with good GNP growth we see growth of airline passenger miles substantially above GNP growth because there has been a systematic long-term tendency for airline passenger miles to grow faster than GNP. We can look at the present situation as one in which a number of mistakes were made three to five years ago in putting in capacity too soon, and what we can see is a phasing out of the excess capacity (excess capacity which has come about partly from mistakes in forecasting and partly from too much regulation) and a phasing in of the growth of new demand so as to prevent the occurrence of the loss of a significant number of airlines through the addition of competition. We forecast that some airlines will be made considerably better off by opening up entry and by rate flexibility, and some will be made worse off. But because the phasing occurs over a ten-year period, we believe it is not likely that there will be any substantial losses to particular lines that can be laid to regulatory reform.

HEALTH CARE REGULATION

The session on health care regulation began with a discussion by Professor H. E. Frech III of reforms he advocates to stimulate competition in the medical care industry and improve the position of the consumer. Professor Paul Ginsburg followed with a detailed look at the effects of regulation on the quantity, quality, and efficiency of hospital care.

H. E. FRECH III

Regulatory Reform: The Case of the Medical Care Industry

Americans spend over 7 percent of their GNP for medical care, which is more than most nations. But in the United States the level of health measured in terms of life expectancy and disability is noticeably lower than in most industrialized nations that spend less. Furthermore, costs have been rising very rapidly in recent years while health status has improved very little.

This poor performance has led to regulatory changes and pressure for more regulation based largely on the argument that the free market has failed in health care. But the premise of this argument is wrong: health care is not delivered in a free market. It has been heavily regulated for many years and may be the most regulated sector of the economy. If anything, the poor performance of the current health care system is evidence against regulation rather than in favor of it. The observation that markets in health care are imperfectly competitive is not a sufficient argument for regulation, because regulation itself is imperfect. It has costs of its own. More important, the political economy of regulation seems to lead to dominance of providers over consumers in the regulatory process, a regulatory phenomenon that is not unusual in the case of health care.

There are basically two competing hypotheses on the politics of regulation. The first, the consumer-protection hypothesis, holds that regulation benefits the consumer by reducing monopolistic exploitation, compensating for market imperfection, or both. The producer-protection hypothesis holds that regulation serves producer interests, largely by reducing competition. The latter is the newer view, and it has come to dominate scholarly thinking about regulation. The rationale for this producer-protection hypothesis involves the politics of interest groups. The idea is that producers have a continuing strong interest in what happens to regulatory policy and good information about it, whereas consumers have a much smaller interest and are much less likely to be informed and organized. Thus, those with the stronger incentives and the better information are more likely to influence regulatory policy. The evidence seems quite strong that medical care regulation can be characterized in this way, and that it has often aided providers either by directly reducing competition or by aiding private activities of producers that have anticompetitive effects.

Rational analysis has been impeded by the easy acceptance of some popular arguments in favor of regulation. Consumer ignorance of medical technology and of the value the consumer should place on the outcome of a medical procedure is widely believed virtually to prohibit consumer choice in medical care. This argument is used to support regulatory limitations on consumer choice largely in the name of quality, but there are incentives for the market to develop substitutes for detailed consumer knowledge of medical technology. In other industries, firms have developed brand name reputations for quality, advertising has reinforced brand name identity and provided a certain amount of consumer information, and independent quality assessment institutions have arisen, such as Consumers Union and specialized magazines.

There is a side to the information problem that rarely receives the attention it deserves. The informational advantage does not lie entirely with the provider. There are important bits of knowledge that are vital for many rational decisions and that only the consumer has access to. For instance, only consumers can weigh medical care against other goods. The comparison between a little bit more housing and a little bit more medical care is necessarily subjective.

Some of the unrecognized costs of regulation in medical care provide evidence for the hypothesis that regulation often benefits producers over consumers. Take occupational licensure for instance. Licensure tends to reduce consumer information. Virtually all professions try to reduce consumer information where competition is involved (advertising restrictions are probably the most common example of this). Another point about licensure that has not received sufficient attention is that the licensure of physicians has aided organized medicine in its opposition to health maintenance organizations (HMOs). An HMO provides medical care in return for a fixed prepayment. It combines the function of insurer and medical care provider in the same organization. HMOs are important because they develop valuable brand name reputations for quality, thereby improving consumer information, and they do not have the incentives for overuse and overinvestment which fee-for-service medicine has under the presence of insurance. Licensure has made it more difficult for insurers to institute cost controls. This has come to light in some very interesting antitrust court cases. For instance, Blue Shield and the Medical Society of Oregon were sued for using boycott and predatory pricing against private insurers. The defendants submitted a list of insurer cost control practices, calling these unethical interferences in medical care.

Regulation favors Blue Cross and Blue Shield over other insurance companies, and Blue Cross and Blue Shield are strongly influenced by providers, if not completely controlled by them. The Blues use their regulatory advantage to increase the scope of the insurance policies that are sold—they make an individual's insurance more complete. This more complete coverage aggravates the problems of third-party payment, raises prices, and makes the medical care market less competitive.

Regulation of institutional investment, especially hospital beds, by local planning agencies, is relatively new. Nevertheless, we can point to some serious

17

problems with this supply-limiting regulation. First, there seems to be no rational way to calculate what supply should be. The optimal supply depends on the health status, income, and subjective preferences of the population, just to mention three factors. Even more serious is the problem of rationing medical care if supply is limited by regulation. If we use price rationing and allow the price to rise, the price will rise so much that it will almost eliminate the risk reduction benefits of insurance. Further, the increase in revenue for the hospitals is likely to be spent in accord with the preference of hospitals and medical staff, rather than the preference of consumers. On the other hand, non-price rationing leads to important decisions being made without any mechanisms for taking patient preferences into account. Professional preferences, in this case the preferences of the regulators, are again substituted for consumer preferences. There is a real dilemma here. The empirical research on this type of regulation indicates that what is being used is price rationing.

Under state certificate of need laws, a hospital cannot invest in additional patient capacity without getting permission from a local planning agency. In the period 1968–74, states with this kind of regulation experienced 3.4 percent to 9 percent slower growth in beds, but 10 percent to 19.7 percent faster growth in assets per bed than did states without these controls. The net result was no change in investment, but a fairly sizable change in the composition of investment. My interpretation of these results is that the supply restriction allows hospitals to raise their prices, but nonprofit hospitals, of course, do not take the increase in revenue as profit and pay it over to stockholders. Instead they upgrade the style of care that they offer to a style that is considered of better quality or more sophisticated by the hospital and medical staff. Much of this "quality increase" may be in duplication of little-used facilities. However, since under-used facilities often have poorer track records than facilities that are fully used, the new facility may actually lower the overall quality of care in the community from the consumer's viewpoint. Thus, supply-limiting regulation may turn out to lower quality and raise costs—quite the opposite of its intention.

I would like to sketch some ideas for regulatory reform. The first has to do with occupational licensure. I would replace occupational licensure with certification—that is, with labeling those who meet minimum standards—and then allow anyone to work who is certified and can find consumers or employers. Certification provides as much information as licensure, but it avoids some of licensure's unfortunate side effects on efficiency and competition. Certification is now used for some types of engineers, some allied health professions, and by the specialty boards of medicine. Many observers may be willing to go along with certification for all types of health care providers except physicians.

Reuben A. Kessel has proposed some structural changes in the licensure of physicians which are worth considering. He would open up the medical profession to those who pass a performance-based test, regardless of educational background. This is intended to encourage innovation in education and reduce the influence of the organized profession over education. Secondly, Kessel would require all physicians to retake the examination periodically. This would improve quality and information and also eliminate the incentive to use the test as a way of limiting entry into the profession.

Clark C. Havighurst recommends what he calls "the antitrust approach" to medical care. For example, professional restraints on advertising and other information flows would be outlawed, and professional restraints on HMOs and their employees would be illegal. It is not clear whether the application of existing antitrust law to medical care would be sufficient or if new antitrust legislation would be necessary.

As for reform of health insurance regulation, I would eliminate special privileges for Blue Cross and Blue Shield. My research indicates that this would reduce the ability of these firms to induce consumers to buy overly complete insurance. I would also eliminate the tax deductibility for health insurance premiums. This would encourage consumers, especially those in high tax brackets, to buy less than total insurance. Less complete insurance would reduce the demand inflation and inefficiency problems caused by extensive third-party payments.

As for certificate-of-need regulation, I would recommend removing the certificate-of-need powers from planning agencies, because the problems and dangers involved seem to me to be great. I would also take away the power to regulate health maintenance organizations from the planning agencies because HMOs do not have the incentives in favor of overinvestment and overuse that the fee-for-service sector has.

PAUL GINSBURG

Regulating the Price of Hospital Services

Five years ago, we had virtually no regulation of hospital prices, but now we have it in a few states, and I expect that we will see a lot more of it. Given our present system of financing health care—by that I mean the predominance of service-benefit health insurance—price regulation is a second-best solution. There are some very serious problems with it, but it is unlikely that a better solution (basic reform in health care financing) will occur in the near future or proceed rapidly enough to provide relief from the damaging effects of our current financing system.

Dr. Newhouse, who is sitting on the panel, was one of the first to introduce the theory that hospitals have entry barriers and thus have potential monopoly rents. However, since they are not-for-profit organizations, they do not earn high profits to pay out to stockholders. Instead they subsidize the production of more care and of a higher level or quality of care than the market would be demanding. One problem with this theory and others is the meaning of the word "quality." While people generally think of quality as meaning increased or enhanced effectiveness of care, in this context quality frequently stands for the complexity of the services or the prestigiousness of the procedures rather than any real increase in quality of care. For example, a hospital may regard a new open-heart surgery unit as an increase in quality, while medical practitioners tell us that still another open-heart surgery unit can actually decrease the effectiveness of hospital care. Martin Feldstein has shown that an increase in the demand for hospital care, which is caused by increased use of insurance and increased income among the potential patient population, leads to more "quality" and to higher wages for hospital employees than the market would provide. Thus he shows a relationship between demand (or insurance) and the costliness of hospital care through this mechanism of "quality." There are alternative explanations, but the work of economists on the theory of hospital behavior has concentrated on the variables of output and quality.

In none of these models is technical inefficiency on the part of the hospital management considered. There are indications, however, that hospital efficiency is not at the optimal level and is an important policy variable. As a result, I have introduced a variable for what I call "managerial slack," which is my way of talking about inefficiency. Included in this variable are payments to hospital employees either in cash or in kind—like perquisites, office space, and so on— above those necessary to retain them, as well as the use of superfluous labor, and the absence of search activity on the part of managers for efficient production techniques.

In 1975, some 90 percent of hospital expenditures were paid by third parties. If real income rises, this percentage will probably rise with or without national health insurance. Indeed, an overwhelming majority of individuals will probably have insurance which covers them in full for hospital services and thus have no incentive to take price into account. This trend will continue to inflate hospital costs, with increases in "quality" up to technological limits and probably high increases in managerial slack as well. For this reason, virtually all of the proposals for national health insurance pending in the Congress call for "perspective reimbursement," which really is a particular type of price regulation. A number of states are experimenting with this system at the present time.

Under the assumption of complete third-party coverage and assuming that the marginal cost of hospital care will not increase with output, the imposition of regulation (which would be equivalent to a fall in the price level) should reduce both the quantity and "quality" of care and have an indeterminate effect on managerial slack. This analysis shows how important it is to set the price properly because the regulated price affects these three important policy variables. We do not know the relationship between price and slack. Moreover, because managerial slack is very costly to measure and detect, it may not be feasible to learn what this relationship is.

We are interested in the quantity of output, its quality, and the level of efficiency with which the care is produced. However, we only have one instrument, the regulated price, to affect these. We cannot achieve an optimal level of all three target variables just by setting the regulated price correctly. For example, we may decide that the level of quality is too low. If want to raise the level of quality through increasing the regulated price, the level of outputs and the level of slack will also rise. We can then accept the trade-offs and compromise among our goals, or we can bring in other regulatory tools such as certificates of need to affect the quantity of care, utilization review to do the same, or professional standards review organizations to affect the quantity or the quality of care. We must be made aware that when we begin regulating hospital prices, there is a tendency to bring in other types of regulation. It is unlikely that we would be able to regulate price and leave hospital care otherwise unregulated.

A number of practical difficulties must be faced in considering the regulation of hospital prices. First, we have great difficulty in measuring the output of a hospital. A day in hospital "A" is often different from a day in hospital "B." Even more troublesome, a day in hospital "A" in 1975, may be very different from a day in that same hospital in 1980. The second problem is that hospitals do specialize as far as types of output they produce. A payment unit has to be chosen—that is, a unit of output on which we base what the hospital should be paid. None of the payment units are neutral with regard to length of stay. For instance, using patient days gives incentive to increased length of stay, while using patient admissions gives an incentive to reduced length of stay. What this really shows is that there is another variable we have to worry about, that output is not a single variable but rather made up of two—the admission rate and the average length of stay. This adds a fourth policy or target variable that we have to manage with the one tool, regulated price.

Another task is to choose a rate-setting mechanism. We cannot pay all hospitals the same rate, because their outputs are different and some of the factor prices they pay are different. One solution would be to employ uniform percentage increases from a base. This was the system used in the economic stabilization program. This type of rate setting allows both legitimate and illegitimate costs into the system, and it is not very useful over the long run because prices in the base year eventually become irrelevant. An alternative rate-setting mechanism is the cost function approach. This allows costs to vary on the basis of factors that the regulators choose to monitor and are able to incorporate into the cost function. This approach would have the advantage of not unwittingly rewarding low productivity hospitals, but the disadvantage of not being able to take into account all factors that might influence the rates.

An interesting question is, "Who will dominate the rate-setting process from a political-administrative point of view?" It has certainly been the experience in many other areas of regulation that the regulated industry has come to dominate the regulatory process and this would probably hold true in the hospital industry. But even if the process did become dominated by the hospital industry, the results could turn out better than they would from continuing our present system of complete third-party coverage with no restrictions at all on how high hospital costs can rise.

There is also the possibility that the process would not be dominated by the hospital industry. There might be an important countervailing force that has not occurred in other industries because government finances a large part of hospital expenses through taxes. If hospital costs were to continue to increase at a rapid rate, there would be less government money to spend on other programs, or taxes would have to be raised. Unlike other industries where the consumer can wind up suffering from industry domination of the regulatory process, in health care government officials may provide an effective countervailing force.

There are alternatives to rate setting. One would be to continue the current financing system with third-party payment and cost reimbursement.

Under the national health insurance system in Canada, which is essentially an open-ended cost reimbursement system for hospitals, there are tremendous transfers from the taxpayers to the employees of hospitals.

Another alternative would be major reform in the way hospital care is financed. Financing reform would treat the causes rather than the symptoms of hospital cost inflation by giving the consumer and provider incentives for cost containments compatible with protection against financial catastrophe and subsidization of health care for the poor. One possibility for this reform would be the HMO, where the patient or the government pays an annual fee for a specified range of services to be delivered as needed, with the need determined by the physicians. Since, with the HMO, the gross revenue obtained by the physicians is fixed, there is an incentive to limit utilization and use preventive care when effective. By combining the provider of services and the insurer of services into one organization, the age-old problem of "moral hazard" that we find with traditional forms of health insurance is avoided.

HMOs are growing, and they tend to be favored by both liberal and conservative academicians. However, they are opposed by organized medicine. The HMO is an excellent solution, but it is very much a long-run solution. Currently, about 5 percent of patients are served by HMOs, and since the group practice model of the HMO appears to be favored at present, one can see that it will take many years before a substantial part of the population is covered by HMOs. We cannot wait for this to occur.

Another financing alternative would be to change the incentives of the consumers of health care. Proposals for this include use of indemnity insurance in which the insurance policy is denominated in terms of a certain number of dollars per day of hospital care, rather than the complete costs. This would give consumers and their physicians some incentive to avoid the high-priced hospitals. There is a similar proposal to have large deductibles in health insurance, but the tax deductibility of health insurance premiums probably prevents a move in this direction. With an extensive tax subsidy, it is unlikely that people would voluntarily switch from full coverage insurance to other types which might be less inflationary in the hospital sector. I do not think this tax loophole would be given up . . . it is enjoyed by too many people for that. Thus in the short run, I think, we are faced with the prospect of regulating hospital prices as a second-best solution.

Regulating the price of hospital services involves many philosophical and technical problems. Regulation will probably cause distortions in the production of hospital services and the regulatory procedure may be dominated by the hospital industry. Despite this, it may be the most feasible instrument to deal with the problem of chronic inflation in hospital costs caused by third-party financing of hospital care with service benefit insurance.

Commentaries

RITA RICARDO CAMPBELL: Controlling medical care prices is difficult, but controlling total costs is virtually impossible with cost equal to the price times the utilization rate. However, if (as some who favor national health insurance propose) prices per item were eliminated and a negotiated prospective per capita charge—in place of physician fees—and prospective costs—in place of itemized charges—were used to reimburse hospitals, then total costs could be negotiated a year ahead. For this to result in relative cost stability over the long run would be unlikely and would depend on the negotiators. This year-ahead budget approach raises the ethical question of who in society should decide what percent of gross national product should be spent on health—whether 8 percent as in the United States, 5 percent as in Great Britain, or some other "optimum" figure pulled out of the air.

During Phase II of the recent price controls, the Health Services Industry Committee developed a complex system that did successfully control prices —at least, that controlled them relative to prices in the other sectors of the economy. This committee could not, however, control utilization, and physicians became adept at breaking out different medical procedures and items and charging separately for procedures that previously were included in an overall charge. Phase II was successful only in a limited fashion and viable only as a short-run device because of two conditions that cannot be anticipated to hold in the long run: voluntary compliance by providers and a conscious use of delay in decision making by the regulators.

An expressed aim of government regulation in this field is to increase the accessibility to medical care for those individuals who do not have ready access today. Since Medicare and Medicaid pay a large part of the medical care bills of the aged and poor, it is primarily one segment of the population that appears to have limited accessibility to medical care, a segment including children, those who live in rural areas, and migrant workers. Even though they are employed, many persons in rural areas do not have group health insurance coverage from their employers, and the supply of physicians in rural areas is limited. It is not clear how existing government regulation or a financially oriented national health insurance can help this situation.

Although all western European nations have some form of government program either to provide or to finance health care, the same problems of rapidly rising costs and lack of availability to rural populations exist in Europe as exist here. This occurs even though each of these programs has unique characteristics. The rate of increase in annual health expenditures in recent years has in most countries been greater than in the United States, even when inflationary factors are accounted for. Utilization increase and inflationary pull in prices coupled with maldistribution of supply are common to all countries, regardless of the system of health care and its financing. Professor Frech's option of planned deregulation to increase competition is, from my experience, the preferred solution, although not all of his solutions or suggestions can be accepted as politically viable.

Neither national health insurance nor government regulation can correct or dampen the basic reasons for exploding health costs: (1) the third-party payments, (2) the rigidities of supply; (3) the fact that medical technology is increasingly expensive and does generally not cure but rather provides supportive care; (4) the noncompetitive markets that exist partly because informational feedback is lacking and prices are not present to allocate the resources; (5)

and possibly most important, consumers that have over-expectations as to medical cures.

JOSEPH NEWHOUSE: The two authors of these papers have some common themes that appear in other sessions at this conference—most notably, that regulation has not worked well in other industries because the regulated have a strong incentive to try to manipulate regulation and there tends to be asymmetry of information and asymmetry of incentives between the regulators and consumers. In other words, consumers have difficulty organizing and regulators have their own agenda for stability or the quiet life or whatever. All of this tends to lead to barriers to entry, resistance to technological change, potential cartelization, and a general anticompetitive stance. Implicit in that criticism is the view that competition for the consumers' business on the basis of price is a very good method and perhaps the best feasible method of achieving the goals of producing what the consumers want in an efficient fashion. The view that price competition is a good thing is often questioned when it is applied to medical care: very distinguished persons have held that in this area competition and consumer sovereignty are inappropriate, in large part because they conflict with equal access to medical services based on medical need.

The authors of the two papers share a distrust of regulation, but they come to rather opposite conclusions. Professor Ginsburg believes that the financing mechanism precludes competition on the basis of price in the short run, and therefore the analytical problem to be solved is what may be the best way to regulate price. Professor Frech would deregulate generally. They agree, however, that HMOs and the fee-for-service system should be put on equal footing, but though I think the case for doing that is a compelling one, I am not sure it will lead to a lot more price competition.

First, many people do not want HMOs to compete with each other on the basis of price, in part because of the goal of equity. Second, even if HMOs do compete on the basis of price, given what we know about what consumers have chosen in the past, it is not obvious that when faced with a price differential involving HMOs consumers would choose the less expensive form of health care. I think a more important and fundamental problem is the possibility of adverse selection—that is, there will be an incentive for anyone who has expected expenditures less than the average for his group to look for a different group with lower average expenditures. This would tend to fragment groups and might render the possibility of competing HMOs impossible. In addition, about a third of the country lives in rural areas, and a viable HMO competing with either another HMO or the fee-for-service system is not a likely possibility in such an area.

Professor Frech, Professor Ginsburg, and I agree that the tax treatment of health insurance premiums should be changed. I think the current deduction, regardless of one's goals, is a rather inefficient kind of instrument. But even if the tax subsidy were reformed or eliminated, I am not sure that a significant amount of price competition would result.

Professor Frech recommends putting the "Blues," the commercial insurance companies, and the independent health and welfare plans on equal footing.

If the goal is to have an efficient private insurance industry, that recommendation is quite unobjectionable, but I do not think it would lead to price competition in hospitals. Professor Frech also suggests better claims review by the insurance companies. My instinct is that the costliness of trying to review claims and disallow them is sufficiently high that the companies choose not to do it.

I am less optimistic than Professor Frech and Professor Ginsburg about the possibilities of competition in health care on the basis of price. I think that there is a challenge for analysis so that we may assess the feasibility of greater competition on the basis of price and what its effects would be.

STUART ALTMAN: This country now spends in excess of $120 billion a year on health care and related activities. The figure is growing at the rate of 14 to 15 percent a year. In the four years that I have been in my job, health care costs have risen by $50 billion. We are looking at an industry that is fast approaching 10 percent of our GNP.

The federal government spends $30 billion a year on health programs. Next year alone, we estimate that our Medicare and Medicaid programs will increase by more than $4 billion. The issue we have to face is whether these rates of increase are of such magnitude and are causing such distortions (not only in what the federal government spends but also in what businesses and individuals are spending for health insurance premiums and health care) that something needs to be done. We must begin to think along the lines Paul Ginsburg laid out. Reluctantly, we are going to get into the business of controlling expenditures and rates of increase. We cannot get there from here just by permitting more advertising, giving consumers more education, increasing the proportion of health care provided by HMOs from 3 percent to 6 percent, introducing physician extenders, introducing some increases in cost sharing, and ending the tax subsidy for health insurance.

This industry is unlike the airline industry and unlike the natural gas industry in one very important respect. The federal and state governments are major purchasers of health care. They spend close to $50 billion a year on health care. If anyone thinks that does not matter in preventing provider domination, he should have been part of the economic stabilization program. My more serious concern is that we could, through regulation, see a totally planned and government-run health system. I would much rather see a regulated system than a system planned and totally dominated by government, be it state or federal.

I predict that this country is going to make a political decision in favor of increasing regulation. I hope that it is done in a constructive and intelligent way. The real issue at stake in the health industry is whether we are going to allow the current system to continue, or make some major changes in the way we reimburse providers—recognizing that, in doing it, we are going to create a lot of bureaucratic slack and a lot of the other bad things that have been mentioned.

PHILIP CAPER: Very little reference is made in these papers to social and distributional justice as it applies to health care or to the ethical or moral questions raised by the question of universal entitlement to health care services.

Health care is not and should not be considered a commodity, perceived to be the same in kind as other goods and services. Health care is not governed by marketplace economics. People consider health services to be qualitatively different from other goods and services. The existence of national health insurance plans in virtually every developed country—with the exception of the United States—and the existence of a strong, persistent drive toward national health insurance in this country is, I believe, evidence of that.

There are references in both papers to the differences between the health care industry and the classic free enterprise marketplace. One of the major differences is that the purchasers of health care services do not, by and large, make purchasing decisions. Purchasing decisions are made almost exclusively by physicians, not by patients. The patient's ability to discriminate between alternatives is largely circumscribed by the advice he receives from his physician. Within this framework, it is not difficult to understand why the free-market fantasy, projected for the health care industry by some scholars, cannot and will not ever exist. The alternative, regulation of some kind, is already firmly entrenched. Growth of regulatory activity seems to me inevitable.

Throughout both papers attempts are made to introduce the concept of quality into the author's economic formulations as an essential variable, but one that is very difficult to measure. My impression is that the magnitude of the difficulties inherent in evaluating the quality of medical care is understated and perhaps underappreciated. The primitive state of the art is astounding when we come to evaluating the effectiveness of what are frequently costly, highly complex, diagnostic and therapeutic procedures.

A very important change in society's expectations from physicians is under way. In the past physicians have always been expected to do their utmost for their patients, and now technologic improvements have significantly increased the physician's effectiveness in treating disease. The proliferation of third-party coverage has made costs to the individual at the time of the illness relatively unimportant. As a result of the rise in total expenditures for health care, together with the intervention of the federal government as the single largest purchaser of health care services, society is imposing an additional and conflicting requirement upon physicians—that they be socially responsible and voluntarily limit the services they provide their patients, even though such limitation may directly conflict with their training and their perception of what is best for their patients. In my opinion, this conflict is inevitable. It will be resolved not through an academic or a scientific process, but rather through a political one.

If the rate of increase in expenditure for health care services continues as it has in the recent past, some limitation will have to be imposed on total national health expenditures. As pressures to contain costs mount, it will become increasingly important to develop ways of measuring the quality of medical care as defined by its effectiveness in modifying the course of illness, alleviating pain, reducing disability, and prolonging life. No economic analysis of the health care industry is complete without careful attention to that bottom line.

Within the context of a limitation on overall expenditures for health care services, questions of equity and effectiveness must be asked. One of the preliminary conclusions of Dr. Newhouse's work is that a national health insurance program, if enacted at the present time, would increase demand, particularly in the ambulatory care sector, and result in queuing. I believe that consideration should be given to the equity of queuing as opposed to the ability to purchase health care services as a utilization control device.

Professor Frech makes the point that a stretching of supplies, such as would be inevitable if total expenditures were restricted, would result in increased price. I believe that increased price may be acceptable if it is accompanied by a reduction in marginally effective or unnecessary services and a consequent stabilization of total national expenditures.

I believe that whether the health care industry should be regulated or allowed to function as a free-market endeavor is a moot question. It is currently regulated and will be more heavily regulated in the future. In addition, I believe that increasing total national expenditures for health care will result in some sort of de facto or de jure ceiling upon total national expenditures for health care. Attention will then shift to questions of social equity and access to health care services within a no-longer-limitless health care sphere, and to ways of improving the quality or efficiency of health care in alleviating pain and suffering, reducing morbidity, and prolonging life.

TRANSPORTATION REGULATION

In the session on transportation regulation, Dr. Thomas G. Moore reviewed the administration's proposed Railroad Revitalization Act. He advocated deregulation of the railroads that would lead in the long run to a highly competitive transportation system having five or six nationwide railroads authorized to own motor carriers and water carriers and unrestricted in either the commodities or the places they could serve. Next, Dr. James C. Miller III discussed the prospects for substantial reform of domestic airline regulation and outlined the case for the administration's reform proposal.

THOMAS GALE MOORE

The Proposed "Railroad Revitalization Act"

In May, the Ford administration sent to Congress a bill entitled the Railroad Revitalization Act. I want to discuss the question whether this bill will revitalize the railroads and to suggest some ways in which the bill might be strengthened practically.

The first substantive section of this bill makes abandonment more difficult than it is now. It provides additional protection to workers by guaranteeing their job security for four years, which effectively means that most abandonments would be prevented. We need more rather than less abandonment. A number of studies have indicated that there is excess capital in the industry, especially in the form of tracks. Some 21,000 miles or 10 percent of the present rail network has been estimated by the Federal Railroad Administration to be very light density lines of twenty-five carloads or less annually. The Penn Central found that the 3,000 miles of these branch lines, which are used the least, accounted for only $2 million of its estimated $20 million loss due to excess trackage. The other $18 million stemmed from the remaining 2,000 miles of lines that were low density but used regularly. These low density lines are the lines that are currently serving shippers who are going to oppose their abandonment. The administration bill does not really deal with this important problem. A good bill would permit the railroads to abandon, but it would provide some subsidy aid if there would be severe losses to a community. The administration bill permits cities, communities, states, or shippers to subsidize a line that a railroad wants to abandon. This is not an adequate answer if the shipper had invested in the belief that the railroad was going to continue to operate that line, relying on federal policy, and then the line were abandoned. The shipper might then go bankrupt, not being able to subsidize the line. It would be equitable and efficient for the federal government to provide a subsidy for (say) five years to any line that the railroads wish to abandon because of losses, if it could be shown that the substitution of truck transportation would still leave shippers in poor condition. One efficient way to permit the railroads to get out of some loss operations would be to permit them to go into the trucking business and serve the communities with trucks and piggyback operations in exchange for permission to abandon the lines.

Sections three and five of the proposal are major steps forward. They are intended to produce rate competition and more flexibility in rate making. Section three would limit the role of the rate bureaus in price fixing of joint rates for through traffic. The railroads could no longer get together as they now do and agree on rates. Section five would establish a zone of reasonableness in which a railroad would be free to price without fear of suspension by the commission, except on grounds that the proposed rate was discriminatory, unduly preferential, unduly prejudicial, or that it violated the long-haul and short-haul provisions of the Interstate Commerce Act. A rate could not be suspended on the grounds that it exceeded a just and reasonable level or that it was below a just and reasonable level, provided the rate was within the specified margins. For the first year, the margins would be 7 percent up and down, for the second year, 12 percent, and for the third, 15 percent. After the third year, no rate decrease could be suspended for being unreasonably low and increases of up to 15 percent could not be suspended for being unreasonably high. The commission could suspend general rate increases or rates challenged under sections two, three and four of the Interstate Commerce Act. This proposal would limit the commission's suspension power only. The ICC could still find rates unduly high or unduly low, but this amendment would provide the railroads with some price flexibility. At least for a period of time, they could test out new rates.

Probably the best evidence of what would happen to rates under these provisions comes from some European experience. West Germany, for example, went from a system of fixed rates in trucking to a system of bracket rates or margin rates similar to those in the administration proposal. Most of the rates there have tended to move near the bottom of the margin. During a one-year period, only 0.4 percent of the ten ton shipments moved at rates above the regular tariff. The bulk of the rates, as one would expect, went down. It must be acknowledged that the West German experience in trucking may not parallel the U.S. experience in railroads. It is clear that there are many more trucking firms competing in West Germany than there are railroads competing in a given market in the United States. On the other hand, there is considerable competition among the railroads themselves for long-haul shipping, and they face competition from trucks in short haul. The additional competition from rate flexibility should permit the railroads to continue the trend toward specializing in bulk commodities and piggyback operations.

Section nine of the bill provides for loan guarantees to railroads. The provisions tend to be inconsistent with each other. They seem to be a substitute for going directly to the treasury, but they amount to an equal drain on the capital markets. The bill also has a provision for railroad restructuring that permits the secretary of transportation to condition these loan guarantees on the restructuring of the rail system. The idea is to encourage mergers and consolidations while reducing excess trackage and duplicate facilities. Ostensibly, the mergers will be voluntary, but of course the loan guarantees could be withheld if the mergers did not take place. My primary objection here is that the bill seems to be aimed at promoting parallel mergers. We have had some experience with parallel mergers; indeed, we are all familiar with the debacle at the Penn Central. It is not clear that other parallel mergers will not have the same result. Some studies have shown that mergers, especially parallel mergers, have resulted in very little cost saving, and many have added to cost. The basic problem with parallel mergers is that they achieve no economies of scale.

There is a kind of merger that could be helpful. The task force on railroad productivity recommended end-to-end mergers to promote a series of nationwide railroads to compete with each other. They envisioned four, five, or perhaps six strong nationwide railroads operating from coast to coast and from the northern to the southern border. End-to-end mergers would reduce the cost of interlining. They would reduce the car shortage program which is compounded by one railroad's hoarding the cars of another because with nationwide railroads most of the time the cars would stay on their own tracks. The nationwide railroad could operate the whole network as an efficient unit, and it would be able to offer the shipper continuous service and to guarantee the service throughout the network.

Of course, it is easy to envision five nationwide railroads, but how do we get them? The first step is to clear up the problem of the Penn Central. Perhaps the Penn Central could be subdivided into two railroads along the lines of the old Pennsylvania and the old New York Central. The Northeast corridor could be sold off to Amtrak which now operates it for passenger operations. To make this subdivision work, all the light density lines that the Penn Central is stuck with should be abandoned. Of course, this would be very difficult to do politically. The communities that would be cut off will bring pressure to bear, but we will have to bite the bullet to provide an efficient system of nationwide railroads. The other possible disadvantage of this proposal for nationwide carriers is that there may be diseconomies of scale, and that the railroads will grow too large. The Penn Central downfall is an example of what can happen when a railroad grows too large. However, it seems to me that a large nationwide railroad may be able to operate much more efficiently than a large railroad operating within a region. The Canadian experience with nationwide railroads is very encouraging.

The railroads should be permitted to enter the field of door-to-door service by operating trucking lines. We could have door-to-door service with five railroads operating nationwide with trucking operations to pick up the shipments. We could then have an extremely efficient transportation system. This would be the railroad optimum, with each region of the country served by several railroads. Railroads would be free to abandon traffic whenever it was uneconomic, with provision for subsidies when this abandonment adversely affected communities or shippers, provided that truck transportation could not substitute. If we do not move in this direction we will be moving toward nationalization of the railroad industry. We have heard proposals to nationalize the tracks of the railroad industry with the analogy given of trucks driving on public highways. This track nationalization would subsidize one part of the railroad industry. It would inevitably mean higher cost because there would then be no optimization of the use of tracks and cars. Railroads would ignore the impact of heavy cars on the tracks; the tracks would not be maintained in a way that is optimum for the traffic going over the tracks. Inevitably, the pressure would build to nationalize the rest of the railroad industry. I suggest that the only way that we will avoid nationalization and huge subsidies such as those in Europe is to restructure the railroads into a competitive nationwide system.

JAMES C. MILLER III

Major Issues and Recent Developments in the Airline Deregulation Debate

Times are changing airline regulation. President Ford has indicated that he will send to the Congress very shortly a bill for substantial reform of the regulation of airlines by the Civil Aeronautics Board. The Congress has been very active in this area; in particular, Senator Kennedy's Subcommittee on Administrative Practice and Procedure has circulated a draft report calling for gradual elimination of the CAB's power to regulate the airlines. The CAB itself has announced a proposed deregulation experiment. It has ended the route moratorium, dropped its proposal to establish minimum fares for charter carriage, rejected certain fare increases, and ended existing capacity agreements. Perhaps most spectacularly, the CAB special staff has published a report calling for the elimination of CAB controls over airlines. Coming from within the board, that is most remarkable. I think it is a tribute to the scholarship and the objectivity of that staff.

The public is acutely aware of the rapid fare increases over the past few years, and knows generally of the situations in Texas and California where intrastate carriers have been charging lower fares than have CAB regulated carriers. There have been stories of illegal campaign contributions involving nearly all the major air carriers, and improper conduct has been alleged on the part of some CAB members. A lot of freshmen in Congress are skeptical of the established way of doing business. Committee realignment has taken place in the House, and campaign donation and spending reform has been enacted that makes organized groups like airlines relatively less powerful in the eyes of the members of the House and Senate. Consumers are coming around to supporting deregulation. I imagine it is quite exceptional for a consumer group to think that less regulation will make the consumer better off, but a lot of us who have studied this question firmly believe that. And political leaders are now willing to spend some political capital on this question of regulatory reform.

In the airline industry, entry has been blocked and exit has been blocked, at least for some kinds of carriers. There has been virtually no price competition. What we have had is service competition. The law forbids the CAB from regulating the frequency of service, and carriers have therefore competed on the basis of service frequency, giving us excess capacity. Since they have competed so effectively on service, the airlines have not realized excess profits. We have a lot of empty planes flying around with people paying high fares. Various estimates have been made on the cost of this—one reasonably good estimate is in the neighborhood of a billion dollars a year in dead-weight welfare loss. This is not money the airlines are putting in their pockets that would otherwise stay with consumers; instead it is a situation analogous to one's having a billion dollars of resources, taking it out to the middle of the ocean, and sinking it. The airline market has the preconditions for effective competition: no scale economies, difficulty of coordination in the absence of the CAB, fairly elastic firm demand, and so on. The evidence from the intrastate and commuter markets indicates that unregulated markets will work well.

An important argument invoked against deregulation is that under deregulation there would be wholesale abandonment of markets. Particularly important has been the Air Transport Association's recent study circulated to every congressman showing which routes would be deleted under deregulation. There have been numerous criticisms of that study: for one thing, it seems to rest on the proposition that the carriers would like to delete a lot of markets that they cannot delete, and that is not true. There are in fact a number of markets they could delete that they do not. For another thing, the study seems to rest on the notion that there is substantial cross-subsidy—that some markets produce excessive revenue that subsidizes markets where there are losses. In our study, George Douglas and I found very little evidence of cross-subsidy. It turned out, instead, that allegedly losing markets were getting very poor and thus less expensive service. Moreover, air routes are part of a system, and airlines pick up passengers at one location to feed them into other routes that cover longer distances. After we made the appropriate attributions for cost, taking into account the feeder function, we did not find cross-subsidy. Finally, on this abandonment problem, existing CAB-regulated carriers could be replaced by more efficient carriers in certain markets—even though an existing carrier might want to abandon a market, it does not follow that another carrier would not want to replace him. At College Station, Texas, for example, Texas International was serving markets to Dallas and to Houston. Davis Airlines, an unregulated commuter airline, was offering better service and began taking nearly all of the passengers. The CAB finally allowed Texas International to drop College Station upon a finding that while Davis was making money serving these markets, Texas International was losing $42 per in-plane passenger, with the CAB (and thus the taxpayers) making up the difference. If we count the markets in the United States served by commuter airlines and other airlines, we find that 32 percent of the cities are served exclusively by commuter airlines, 38 percent are served exclusively by certificated carriers, and 30 percent are served jointly.

Some have argued that increased concentration would result from deregulation, but in fact there are no significant scale economies in the airline industry. Even if greater concentration did result, as long as we maintained a policy of free entry (since there are no real economic barriers to entry), concentration would not be much of a problem. Some have argued that rates would be too high as a result of deregulation. But I found that commuter airlines charged lower prices for comparable distances than those charged by the certificated carriers. And there is the argument that rates could be too low as a result of deregulation. Now perhaps until they learned how to operate within a free-

32

enterprise environment, air carriers might do crazy things, but I somehow do not think we would find much evidence of excessively low prices.

The final major argument against deregulation is that the adjustment process would be traumatic. I think the adjustment process could be handled by a phasing program—and that leads me to the administration's air proposal. The proposal would afford flexibility to the airlines for price competition for the first time since 1938 by authorizing a zone that would expand gradually in order for the carriers to compete on price within limits so they could gradually find where the competitive marketplace would place fare levels. There would be prohibitions against predatory pricing on the down side, and CAB control over maximum rates would be retained on the up side. The proposal would also eliminate certain restrictions on providing service. Many times a carrier will propose new service to the CAB, and the CAB will say, "Okay, you can provide the service, but on your way from New York to Los Angeles, you have to stop in Tucson." The bill would gradually eliminate restrictions of this nature, thereby allowing a significant amount of entry. At the end of five years this would result in carriers being able to serve directly between any two cities they now serve, with intermediate stops. There would also be some discretionary entry, with carriers allowed to enter certain markets of their own choosing without formal CAB approval. Moreover, carriers would be permitted to exit quite easily from markets that have competition. Where there is no other existing service, the standard would be strict to protect communities, but exit would be easier than at present. Of course, we should have a strong standard on mergers to make sure that the CAB does not use its merger authority to regain some of the regulatory authority taken away by this proposal. If the bill were passed intact, I do not think mergers would be especially troublesome because free entry would preserve competition. Finally, the administration's proposal would rule out capacity agreements because they are anticompetitive.

I think this bill would accomplish eventually what many of us would like to see—that is, virtually complete deregulation. It would not get us there immediately; we have to make trade-offs. There are serious learned people who believe that chaos, deteriorating service, and airline bankruptcies would result from deregulation. These people talk to congressmen just as the people who favor deregulation do, and the Congress will consider the arguments of both sides. This bill would allow any airline that is now in financial distress an ample opportunity to get into good shape before the provisions of the bill take firm hold. Our projections are that air traffic will pick up markedly in the next few years with growth in disposable income. By the time these major provisions really take effect, the industry and each carrier should be in a firm position. This proposal should be thought of as an experiment. The Congress could reverse its course if results start going wrong. This proposal is different from the CAB's experiment because under that experiment the incentives are strong for each carrier to make the experiment fail. I will not say that this proposal is my first-best solution, but it seems to me that this is a compromise that will get us where we want to go but also meets the objections of those who say that deregulation would be contrary to public interest.

Commentaries

GEORGE JAMES: Dr. Miller cites four reasons for the reversal in the outlook for deregulation. He mentioned the fact that fares have gone up 20 percent in the past two years, the performance of Southwest Airlines, illegal campaign contributions, and the improper conduct of certain CAB officers. None of these reasons relate to any need for deregulation: they merely provide an explanation for the progress that advocates of deregulation have been making. But these advocates are making this progress as a result of the hoax that deregulation will bring lower fares and more efficient operations. I think we have produced a tremendous amount of evidence to the contrary that I would be willing to submit to anyone who would like to see it as we have submitted it many times before. Our fares are markedly lower on a per-mile basis than are foreign carrier fares. Air fares have increased at a much lower rate than have most other prices in the economy over the past twenty years. Moreover, the average cost of airline purchases of all goods and services over the past year has risen 15 percent, and over the last two years, our fuel costs alone have risen over 130 percent. I cannot believe that if we had been deregulated during this period, those costs could have been absorbed. I cannot believe that in the future inflation will completely disappear, and we will be able to get lower fares. On the question of efficient operations, I think we have an outstanding record. We have 3.5 percent fewer employees today than we did in 1969, yet our passengers have increased some 20 percent, and our revenue passenger miles are up some 30 percent over the same period. That is an indication of airline efficiency.

History shows that a primary reason for airline regulation was the provision of public service. Of course, this reason still exists today. Throughout his paper, Dr. Miller assumes that a free market is what we should have. What he should have done is to test airline performance in terms of the adequacy of public service the airlines have provided. He should ask whether adequate public service will continue under deregulation. I think we have a complete misunderstanding on the part of the academic economists about the need and importance of public service and the loss of public service that we would experience under deregulation. Our estimates are that between 22 and 37 percent of the total number of routes we now serve are unprofitable and would be candidates for abandonment under deregulation. It is strange to me that the economist is overlooking this entirely, particularly since Adam Smith, the father of laissez-faire, argued that the state should provide public works as may be necessary to facilitate economic activity when such improvements are unlikely to make a profit. The Civil Aeronautics Act of 1938 provides that the CAB shall promote the "development of an air transportation system properly adapted to the present and future needs of the foreign and domestic commerce of the United States, of the Postal Service, and of the national defense." It was also Adam Smith who wrote back in 1776 that "good roads, canals and navigable rivers, by diminishing the expensive carriage, put the remote parts of the country more nearly upon a level with those in the neighborhood of the town. They are, upon that account, the greatest of all improvements."

DANIEL O'NEAL: George James suggested that economists seem more concerned about marketplace purity in the transportation industry than they do about transportation meeting the national goals of this country. We ought to be more concerned about what those goals are and less about whether market purity can be attained. There is also something cavalier about the attitudes of those who appear willing for others to sustain serious losses so that we can test some economic theories. Let me pose a few questions.

Senator Hartke, in a hearing a few weeks ago, raised an important question: "Don't we have to give some consideration for the role of small business in the United States? Should we rely solely on economic power to determine how well one is served?" Another point: In many non-regulated businesses today, where competition supposedly does exist, prices once again are beginning to go up in the face of declining demand or of demand that is not increasing at a very high rate—does this suggest that deregulation may mean higher rates and nothing else?

And another question: Has the alleged inflexibility of the ICC truly been a primary cause of the distressing financial position of the railroads today? Although most economists are strong in their advocacy of deregulation, there are some who question it. Merrill Roberts, who has written extensively in transportation regulation, says, "There is pretty broad agreement that uneconomic pricing is sapping the carriers' financial fiber and wasting the nation's resources. But the general view that regulation is the culprit in spawning or maintaining these aberrations is highly questionable. The rebukes of the ICC commonly concern its cartelization role and particularly undue restraints on price competition. As a railroad complaint, this charge has little substance and merely serves as an excuse for inaction."

Taking a look at Dr. Moore's remarks, I would note that there are some questions whether greater inter-modal integration will lead to more competition. It may reduce the number of carriers competing, and it would not necessarily lead to more containerized traffic going to the railroads. The Canadian railroads, while they do have integration with other modes, do not derive most of their container traffic from their own motor carriers. And I would point out that the cost to the railroads in carrying containerized traffic are apparently not substantially less than the costs to the motor carriers.

On rail restructuring, I tend to agree with Professor Moore's comments that we need to establish competitive systems and that there would be a great benefit from this. But I doubt that loan guarantees would satisfy the railroads' needs. Furthermore, I think that loan guarantees tend to subsidize banks as well as rails, and I don't think we need to subsidize banks. I certainly do not think there ought to be a tie between the loan guarantees and the restructuring of the railroad industry.

PAUL CUNNINGHAM: The two papers have told us that the heat and light of the regulatory reform movement may turn the coal of CAB regulation into the pure and sparkling diamonds of competition. But the heat and light and fire of the regulatory reform movement may also turn the coal of ICC regulation into cold wet ashes. The second conclusion is suggested by Professor Moore's analysis of the DOT bill, and I think it extends to most of the regulatory reform bills. We can see almost immediately that the effects of those bills will at best be limited in scope. We are dealing with marginal reforms of the economic regulatory system, and there is considerable debate on whether or not those are in fact reforms. Of the seven major areas of concern listed in Professor Moore's paper, in only three does he see the administration bill making significant improvements. The restructuring battle is a battle over who should administer the restructuring and not whether it should be done: there is no disagreement on the issue. The question of intermodal integration has not been thoroughly discussed in the public policy field, and probably will not be dealt with immediately. As for the last, the zone of reasonableness, that is dealt with in Senator Hartke's bill in a slightly different way from the way it is dealt with by the administration. From the administration, we have the conclusion that if the DOT bill is adopted, railroad rates will go up and revenues will improve, but it is questionable whether railroads will be able to raise their rates if, as Professor Moore says, they will have to operate in a competitive environment.

Why is there so much noise when the anticipated results are so little? I suggest that this is partially the fault of the economists who have misled us with their analyses. They have not really looked to see where we are allocating our public resources and our private resources. They have not looked to see who wins and who loses, and that is what public policy makers must always look at. The CAB regulatory reform movement may possibly succeed because no one loses except the regulated airlines. Dr. Miller's paper suggests that otherwise nothing is really going to change. Prices will go down, managements will change, and otherwise we will have the same system. Changes in railroad regulation will progress very slowly because many who are affected think they have something to lose from the changes. The resources they fear they will lose may not be immediately identifiable in an economy measured solely by transfer of dollars, but they are real resources and they are represented articulately in the political market. Until economics looks at where those political gains and losses are, I would suggest that the arguments of the economists will not lead the Congress to change the system.

JOHN SNOW: So far the most significant results of the administration's legislative regulatory reform program have been revealed in the rulings, case law, and policy emanating from the regulatory agencies. Viewed from this perspective I think it is clear that the administration's proposed regulatory reform legislation for rails, aviation, and trucks is already bearing fruit. This is gratifying and suggests that the climate is conducive to significant legislative reform.

I am in basic agreement with the economic analysis in the Moore and Miller papers. But I would emphasize that public policy should be concerned with setting the proper economic incentives, and not with forcing the industry into a particular structure. The proper incentive system does not change with time: the optimal industry structure does.

The Miller paper indicates the extent to which economists are in the forefront in helping to develop public policy rather than merely being critics of existing public policy. The only major exception I can take to the Miller analysis is on the estimates of the deadweight welfare loss. These estimated annual losses are highly uncertain and they do not provide the best case for aviation regulatory reform. A more persuasive and also far more important argument against the present regulatory system is that it stifles entrepreneurship and innovation without serving any useful social purpose. In order to preserve the enterprise system, the rights of those to engage in business must not be infringed upon unless there are overwhelming arguments for so doing. The important aspect of the Miller paper is that it shows there is little or no case for limiting the right to engage in the airline business. This argument is much harder to discredit than are the highly speculative numerical estimates of social savings. Moreover, it helps shift the burden of proof to those who advocate regulation. It is much harder to make a positive case for regulation than to attack estimates of social savings.

Discussion

EDMUND KITCH, University of Chicago Law School: There is one topic that has not been mentioned at the table that is an important factor in these industries. That topic is the impact of the preferred position which the labor force in these industries has been able to obtain for itself and the important contribution which the regulatory structure has made to that preferred position. I realize that this issue is not discussed for two quite separate reasons. One is that everyone concludes the problem cannot be dealt with politically, for very obvious reasons, and therefore the best course is simply to try and work around it. The second is that in the academic tradition this is an area for industrial organization economists and not for labor economists. Thus, although there has been considerable analysis of the firm structure in regulation, there has not been much discussion of the organization of collective bargaining in these industries. I think there is a reasonable case to be made that the result of the horizontal merger policy in the railroad industry since 1920 and the effect of the certification system in airlines and trucking has been to convert strikes in these industries into national emergencies. If that is the case, I do not see why any gains regulatory reform produces would not simply be captured by these highly skilled, intelligent, and well-advised groups in the labor force.

I also want to comment about the airlines problem which I think is probably more acute and more serious for us as a nation than the remarks so far would suggest. I would like to begin with the history of railroad regulation, which I think falls into two important phases, and then point out that the airline industry is about to go through a comparable switch from the first phase to the second.

The first phase of railroad regulation was designed to hold prices up in the face of a long-term falling trend. The Interstate Commerce Act of 1887 was in part designed to stabilize the railroad cartels when there was a dramatic downward trend in prices. The railroad industry was technologically innovative and progressive throughout the last half of the nineteenth century, and, moreover, we had a general deflationary policy from the end of the Civil War, so that the real price of the railroad industry to its customers was falling year by year. The managements wanted to hold prices up: they were not able to do it very well by themselves, so they sought and received government assistance.

The trend changed about 1900, both because there was a switch to a general inflationary policy and because the chance for technological change had been fairly well exhausted. The political response by 1910 was to impose price controls on the industry. Between 1910 and the outbreak of World War I, in a time of rising industry costs, no fare increases were approved for the nation's railroad industry. At the outbreak of World War I, the railroad industry was nationalized, and the principal reason for nationalization was that, if the railroad industry operated under direct government organization, it would be able to raise its prices immediately without ICC approval. After the war, it was decided to try to resuscitate the private companies. That decision led to the Transportation Act of 1920 and the beginning of the rescue effort that has continued to the present day. Once an industry becomes involved in a government rescue effort, the politics requires that the industry be largely prostrate for the subsidy program to be sold. The industry has to be broke in order to get the help it needs.

I think we are now seeing the same thing happen in the airline industry. The technological gains appear to be largely completed and the costs over time now appear to be rising. The Civil Aeronautics Board which, from 1938 to 1970, had shown no real interest in regulating prices, has begun to show a serious and systematic interest in the problem of regulating prices. We are now beginning to see a strong interest in holding prices down in the airline industry. This interest in holding prices down in a period of rising costs will demoralize airline management. To make factual determinations about issues that are very difficult to deal with factually takes time. Between 1910 and 1916, the ICC made an effort to find out what the costs of the railroads were. I think the same length of time at least will be needed for the airline industry. During that time the creative management people will die off, and they will not be replaced because such people will not want to go into an industry in this kind of flux. I do not think we will be able to deal with this problem before the airlines are locked in as the railroads were, and then we will spend the rest of the century trying to figure out how to help the airlines.

LUNCHEON ADDRESS

At lunch, Dr. Gary Seevers spoke about the functions and aims of the Commodity Futures Trading Commission, a recently created regulatory agency.

GARY SEEVERS

Lessons for a New Regulatory Commission

I am here as the representative of the newest major regulatory commission in Washington, now only five months old. In that short time, we have not yet caught any of the common afflictions of regulatory agencies. We have so far avoided the legalistic approach to economic regulation, though I fear that may not be true for long. Indeed that legalistic approach is probably unavoidable for regulatory agencies that have statutory responsibilities covering not only executive or administrative functions but also legislative or rule-making functions and judicial functions.

Our commission has not been captured by the industry we regulate. Indeed, I do not know that we could be. While the industry is small—I would guess that there is a full-time equivalent of perhaps 35,000 people employed by the futures trading industry—there are wide divergences of opinion within that industry and between the industry and the various clients it serves.

Our commission has adopted a policy of open procedures and open meetings to encourage input from the general public. Up to now public input to our commission has been meager. I wish we could get one thoughtful consumer advocate interested in the nuts and bolts of our work. Maybe we will; so far, little interest has been shown in our work, and that is understandable, since the commodity futures trading business is esoteric, regulating it is a tedious process, and the basic functions of futures markets are difficult to appreciate.

The purpose of futures trading is to improve efficiency in markets for actual commodities. Actual commodities are traded in numerous ways, ranging from a myriad of isolated two-party transactions all the way to the large centralized markets that have characterized trading in many agricultural commodities— markets like the hog and cattle markets in Omaha. I think that centralized markets where commodities are brought to one place and there is a bidding or auction process are declining in importance and are being replaced by what I would call "telephone markets." Many commodities are traded on a cash or a spot basis, but commodities are also traded for forward or future delivery.

The futures markets are really auxiliary to the cash and forward markets for actual commodities. They are not a substitute for either, and they really could not exist without them. It should be noted that forward contracts and futures are often confused. The essential difference is that a forward contract between two parties presumes delivery, while a futures transaction presumes offset without delivery. Less than one percent of the futures contracts traded are actually carried to delivery.

Futures markets have not prospered in commodities for which price movements are largely dictated by government regulation or by discretionary private pricing practices. There are no futures markets for chemicals, aluminum, or steel, although attempts have been made to establish such markets for them. The New York market for sugar provides a case of governmental regulation having an impact on futures trading. The New York sugar futures contract was relatively inactive until sugar prices ran above government price supports. Now that there is an economic need, there is an active futures market in sugar.

For commodities like sugar that experience frequent and sizable price movements, futures markets serve two essential economic functions. First, they enable individual market participants to reduce the risks caused by adverse price changes of actual commodities which they own or which they intend to buy or sell. By permitting individual commercial firms to reduce and shift risk among themselves and to others, the futures markets improve the efficiency of these firms' operations. Second, they provide an essential arena for competitive price determination. Futures prices are jointly determined with prices in the cash and forward markets for actual commodities. They provide signals for all segments of an industry, even though not everyone actually trades in futures. The futures market is now used as an indicator for setting cash prices of many commodities: it has displaced the cash market as the primary price signal. This makes the futures market an important public institution.

A futures market is really the ultimate competitive market. Practically any business or individual can buy or sell by paying a nominal commission charge. Prices are determined in a public forum, by open outcry, and are widely disseminated. The question naturally arises why the government should regulate such competitive markets.

Futures trading is vulnerable to internal abuse through improper trading practices, price manipulations, market corners, dissemination of false information, and fraudulent practices with customers and their money. As a result, futures markets have tended to be distrusted by producer groups and by the public. Regulation provides a buffer against actions through the political system which could damage or outlaw futures trading. Indeed, trading in one commodity (onions) was made illegal several years ago by an act of Congress. In effect regulation sanctions futures trading and enables the economic benefits of the markets to be realized, so long as regulation itself does not become a deterrent to the effective operation of futures markets.

The primary objective of regulation is to ensure that futures prices accurately reflect supply and demand. From a regulatory standpoint, the Commodity Futures Trading Commission should not care whether commodity prices are high or low, going up or coming down, so long as those prices reflect the market's estimate of supply and demand. A second objective is to make sure competition is fair to individual investors and market participants. In this respect, regulation should serve as an umpire. The danger here is that the commission might enlarge its role to influence the score, to decide who will be allowed on the teams, or even what the final score should be.

As a regulator, I do see a positive contribution from government regulation of futures trading. However, as a former deregulator, I have mixed emotions about the potential for doing good and for doing harm. The standard regulatory pitfalls do not give me great concern. Fixed commission rates are already being phased out. The commission is not restricting entry in any noteworthy way. As of about two hours ago, we approved our first application for a new contract. One of our regulatory functions is to review any new commodity contract, as well as old ones, and we are charged with evaluating whether that contract serves an economic purpose: the ultimate test is whether trading in such a commodity would be contrary to the public interest. This newly approved contract was submitted by the Chicago Board of Trade and would set up a futures market in mortgage certificates backed by the Government National Mortgage Association (GNMA). We also have an application before us for a futures market in treasury bills. I think we want to encourage new ideas like these and our posture should be to promote free and open entry of new ideas in the futures trading field. Exit is also free and open from the service industry associated with futures trading, as is demonstrated by the high failure rate among individuals and firms in the industry—particularly among floor traders.

Our philosophy at the commission and our statute require us to seek what is called the least anticompetitive means of regulation. The industry receives a little protection against antitrust laws, but they do not have an outright exemption. We are quite aware of the need to avoid generating excess paperwork and the need to conduct prompt decision making. Nevertheless, on the negative side, I do see a number of inherent difficulties in this business.

The commission has judicial responsibilities that could become so time-consuming as to crowd out our more general responsibilities of working with the industry to build more effective futures markets. This matter goes well beyond economics, but the costs of due process can become enormous, and the benefits are difficult to measure. The theoretical answer is to conduct our responsibilities in ways that do not generate a burdensome caseload. In practice, this will be difficult because the statute requires us to establish what is called a "customer reparations procedure" for small investor complaints—which could make us a huge small claims court for the commodity industry.

Enforcement policy is my second concern. I think the commission should have a vigorous but contained enforcement effort. If we proceed on the typical course of regulatory agencies, enforcement will become a much greater operation than I think it needs to be. I believe the primary functions of the commission should be informational, educational, and, quite frankly, to work closely with the industry to make needed improvements in futures trading—in other words, to serve more as a catalyst and less as a policeman. An expansive enforcement program generates a climate that runs contrary to this approach.

Enforcement should, of course, be addressed in a benefit cost framework like any other commitment of taxpayers' money. For every dollar invested in enforcement, additional dollars must be spent on hearings and appeals. The ripple effect of adding one more enforcement officer is something like adding five employees to the commission. Of course, as far as enforcement goes, we must "run the crooks out of the business," but we should not be so preoccupied with this activity that we neglect our primary mission.

There is a lot more "pizazz" in enforcement than in most other functions of a regulatory agency. It is a human tendency for elected and appointed officials to like to see what they are doing covered by the media, and enforcement actions tend to receive good coverage. It is also human to want one's carefully designed regulations to be accepted and promptly followed and to flex one's muscles once in a while.

My concerns are not only about our judicial and enforcement responsibilities, but also about the appropriate contribution of the legal profession to the commission's work generally. We started with a Washington staff of 40 carried over from our predecessor agency. Now we have an interim personnel ceiling of 150 in addition to the five commissioners and their staff. Of the growth of 110, some 80 have been in the legal-judicial area, including hearings and appeals, enforcement, and the general counsel's office. This trend is even more ironic when one considers that we are engaged in regulating an economic activity, not a legal one. Most regulatory bodies in the past seem to have erred far more in their economic work than in their legal work.

We are not—and should not try to be—the SEC for commodity futures trading. Successful enforcement efforts in situations such as market manipulation cases (and to prevent those is really the number-one objective) will require as a pre-condition an effective market-surveillance program—surveillance of the markets in their economic functioning, information content, and trading activity. These are not legal functions. To its credit, the commission has already made the decision to give high priority to economic analysis eventually. We have hired twenty-five lawyers and one economist. I think economic analysis is simply essential for a regulatory agency like ours that wants to be effective over the long haul.

In these early days, I think we still have the luxury of deciding how to organize the commission so that we strike the right balance in the contribution of lawyers, accountants, managers, financial analysts, and all the other professions, even economists, in the commission's future. The balance we achieve will determine whether the CFTC becomes just another regulatory agency or a model agency five years from now.

Discussion

H. E. FRECH III: Can you conceive of any situation where someone wants to create a new futures contract which you think is unwarranted?

DR. SEEVERS: We should have a free entry policy for new contracts. However, just because someone wants a contract does not mean there is going to be anyone who wants to trade it. There are a lot of contracts that no one is trading. I think there is a positive role for the commission to play in reviewing new contracts, but the question presents tough issues. There are now five gold contracts, but a couple of these are almost totally inactive. Suppose that the Minneapolis Grain Exchange comes in to us with an application for another gold contract, and suppose three or four other exchanges also do that. There is a fixed amount of gold trading that can go on. These additional exchanges would expand the quantity of trading a little bit, but not much. I think we are dealing here with a natural monopoly and there is a basic question whether proliferating gold contracts is really a good thing for effective gold trading. That is something we will be investigating.

AGENCY FOR CONSUMER ADVOCACY

The session on the proposed agency for consumer advocacy (ACA) or agency for consumer protection began with Professor Roger Noll's discussion of the dilemma facing proponents of the agency. He stated that while the proponents have made a good case that current regulation often works to the detriment of consumers and that an advocate might help consumers, the agency's opponents have successfully shown that the agency itself would impose costs and would produce quite limited results. Nevertheless, Professor Noll believes that on balance, the ACA may benefit the public. Professor Ralph Winter followed with the argument that the proposed agency would aggravate rather than alleviate the problems it addressed and obfuscate and distract from the real remedy—deregulation. Professor Winter contended that the concept of a consumer advocate is fundamentally defective because there is in fact no single consumer interest but a multitude of conflicting consumer interests.

ROGER NOLL

The Dilemma of Consumer Protection

My conclusion, after reading what everyone else has had to say about the consumer advocacy agency, is that I cannot understand why people are so strongly opposed to it or so strongly in favor of it. If I were forced to vote, I would vote for it—because I accept the principal argument for it—that the consumer advocacy agency will promote justice and fairness. It is unlikely, in my opinion, that this particular agency will have much of an effect for good or ill on regulatory outcomes because I believe that the regulatory process is difficult to reform. Admitted that deregulation is clearly called for in certain circumstances, in other cases I think it would be ridiculous even to contemplate it. In any case, no matter how one draws the line between deregulation and reforming the existing system, one should consider the fact that the regulatory process has definite inevitable costs.

The advocates of the agency point to a fact that is not really in dispute: that regulatory agencies have a tendency to favor producer groups, the well-represented groups, more than the general public interest. In economist's terms, the agencies impose sacrifices of consumer welfare that are greater than the gains they confer upon those who are well represented in the process. The critical part of this argument is the belief that the two characteristics, representation and bias, are causally connected. One has to determine the nature of that causal connection and thus have a theory of regulation before one can predict the effect of the advocacy agency. Most of the current theories of regulation predict there will be little or no effect.

44

High school civics textbooks describe regulatory agencies as steadfast advocates of the consumer because they put binding constraints on regulated firms. Under this theory, the agencies are adversaries of the regulated industries, trying to ensure that they perform well. Obviously, in such a world, the advocacy agency would have little or no reason to exist because it would simply duplicate what was already happening. In the professional literature written by economists, political scientists and lawyers, however, almost no one agrees with the civics text as to how agencies operate. One finds only the agencies themselves and a few of those who deal with them holding honestly that the primary effect of regulation is to serve some ephemeral public interest.

The professional literature views the regulatory process as designed for the purpose of helping producer groups at the expense of consumers. Under this theory, a consumer advocate will not change outcomes. As long as the objectives of the regulatory agency are identical to the objectives of one of the interested groups, the agency can sit back, take all the evidence, and act interested when some other group is being represented in the process. When it writes its opinion, the agency can say it was not persuaded by a particular argument because the refutation offered by the interested group was more convincing. Of course, this result cannot be successfully appealed to the courts because the law will be written in such a way as to protect the particular group it is intended to protect. The procedures will be perfect. Everyone will have had their day in court. Nevertheless, the decisions will be the same as if no one had been in court.

The theoretical model that I subscribe to is based on the notion that the members of the regulatory agencies are trying in their own minds to serve a public interest, but that they have an enormously difficult time determining what the public interest is—in part because there are no good indicators they can go by.

The agencies have imperfect success indicators which are represented somewhere in the following list: the size and growth of the agency's budget, the fate of its legislative program, the number of rules it promulgates, the number of cases it decides, the economic health of the regulated industry, the ability to avoid appeals of decisions (particularly successful appeals), and the tone of the press reviews of the agency's performance.

As long as court reversals and legislative reversals are important to the agency, it will have an incentive to decide uncontested issues in favor of whatever interests are represented in its proceedings. This minimizes the resources committed to each case and means an agency can increase its caseload and the size of its regulatory empire. It makes appeal of decisions unlikely. Furthermore, if the represented groups are rational, this process contributes to the economic health in the regulated sector because presumably the industry knows its own self-interest best and will ask the regulators to promote that self-interest. Intervention by a consumer group or any other nonproducer interest will eliminate the agency's incentive to go beyond legislative intent in favoring producer groups by introducing the threat of successful appeal.

The agencies have at their disposal very imperfect information, most of which comes from the industries they regulate. No matter how well represented a consumer group is, essential data on telephone service will come from the

45

telephone company and information on electric service will come from the electric company. Once that monopoly in information exists, the opportunity arises to use it strategically, not so much by withholding important items as by internally organizing information gathering so that a company does not collect potentially self-damaging information.

The advocacy agency would be operating in this same milieu, but it would have slightly different incentives and perceptions of the public interest. Therefore, under the interest-group-aggregation theory of regulatory decision making the advocacy agency would have an effect upon decisions. The consumer advocacy agency would have different incentives and different goals because it would engage in a wider range of activities at a lower level of intensity than does a conventional regulatory agency. It would deal with many agencies, industries, and interest groups simultaneously. Consequently, it would have less reason to work out accommodations with particular interest groups, and interest groups would have small incentive to capture it because it would be less important to them in the long run than the regulatory agency with which they deal on a day-to-day basis.

The advocacy agency like the regulatory agency would have consumers as a natural constituency, but the consumer interests would be more focused on the consumer advocate than on any particular regulatory proceeding because it would be extremely costly (and not rational) for a consumer to follow all the regulatory agencies in Washington along with all the state and local agencies. It is not rational for even a consumerist organization to follow all the regulatory agencies. The advocacy agency would be a focus for consumerist groups and more responsive to them than are the regulatory agencies.

There are two classes of costs to the advocacy agency that have been identified by those who oppose it. One is a set of direct costs. Once we introduce a consumer advocacy agency into the federal establishment, we significantly increase the cost of the regulatory process—by an amount substantially more than the budget of the agency. We do so in three ways: First of all, proceedings would take more time. My research indicates that it takes two or three times longer to decide a case in which there are intervenors than it takes when there are no intervenors. Secondly, represented groups would respond to the presence of an advocate by stepping up their own expenditures on the regulatory process. They would have better presentations since those presentations would be looked over carefully by an adversary group. Thirdly, a higher proportion of cases would be likely to become formal in the first place because there would be an effective advocate on both sides.

The second class of costs that have been identified are indirect systemic costs. One involves the argument that deregulation is the preferred solution to our problems and that the advocacy agency would be an alternative to deregulation. I do not agree with this. The argument for the advocate is not that we would create this agency rather than deregulate but that we must live with regulation in many sectors and this is a way we can make it work better. As long as we are going to regulate, particularly in the standard-setting area, there is a regulatory reform issue that is separate from the deregulation issue. However, if anyone can convince me that the CAB will last longer because I say I favor the advocate, then I will keep quiet about the advocate until we get rid of the CAB.

The second indirect cost alleged is that the agency would destroy voluntary industry performance standards such as those in the home appliance industry. My contention is that voluntary trade associations would have a greater incentive to exist when there is a consumer advocate because the advocate would have to pick its targets carefully and thus would not choose to go after the industries where trade associations promulgated particularly informational rules. A voluntary trade association amounts to a protective defense against federal regulation.

The third argument about indirect cost involves unrepresentativeness. This is, of course, the serious argument against the consumer advocate. The reasons for this claim of unrepresentativeness are that the agency would be too far removed from consumers because they would not elect its leaders or support it in any voluntary sense and that the consumer interest is actually nonexistent because differences in taste, income, age, residence, and other demographic characteristics make consumers too diverse a group to be well represented by a single advocate. The truth of these contentions as theoretical matters cannot be contested. The problem is indeed worse even than the opponents of the advocacy agency suggest. Regulation, in principle at least, is socially desirable when information costs are so large that the consumer has insufficient incentive to make himself informed enough to engage in optimal consumption decisions. As Gordon Tullock has pointed out, exactly this same phenomenon occurs when the voter must determine which candidate and implicitly which public policy to vote for. This is not a dilemma of consumer policy; it is a dilemma of the entire democratic process. Provision of public goods must always diverge from the optimal, whether the public good be public defense, information about a product, or a safety standard. To say that bureaucracy is unresponsive and the political process incapable of finding a unique set of optimum policies is to say very little while saying very much. The argument no more destroys the proposal for an advocacy agency than it supports it since the agencies which the advocate must deal with will always be unresponsive and unrepresentative for the very same set of reasons. Of course, a social arrangement that provides no public goods is even more unresponsive.

We know on the positive side that the agency would have some effect. We know on the negative side that it would impose some cost. But we have no really effective metric to compare the two. We can apply the interest-group-aggregation model of bureaucratic behavior to see what the advocate would be most likely to do. Through a series of somewhat tortured arguments, I have concluded that it would be a very moderate consumer organization—far more moderate than a private one—in the same sense the Environmental Protection Agency is a far more moderate advocate for the environment than are the Friends of the Earth, the Sierra Club, or any one of a dozen other groups. The bureaucratic political process provides an incentive to be moderate. In order to be successful in changing decisions so that it can have an independent and slightly positive effect, the advocacy agency would have to work out accommodations with regulatory agencies. The second thing the advocate would be likely to do, of course, is to behave like regulated firms facing someone who is not represented—that is, steamroller them. In such cases, the ACA could push for big changes in tiny battles. My conclusion is that, for the same reasons that it would have an effect on regulatory agencies, the advocacy agency would have a minimal effect on regulatory outcomes because the bureaucratic incentives operating through Congress, the Executive, and the courts would cause it to be moderate the same way that regulatory agencies are moderate.

RALPH K. WINTER, JR.

What Is in a Name?

I do not think that "should we have an agency for consumer advocacy?" is the same question as "should we have a free market or a regulated market?" Those are not the alternatives.

I recall that when I first testified about this agency, I said that it had a terrific statement of purpose and a fine title. The title then was "Consumer Protection Agency." The agency has been weakened in that the title of the agency has been changed to "Agency for Consumer Advocacy," but that happens to be a far more accurate title for the agency than the previous one, and the sponsors are to be applauded for furthering the goal of truth in advertising. Nevertheless, I have two basic objections to the agency. The first is that it does not seem very well tailored to cure the abuses that have been identified as calling it forth. Those abuses really call for deregulation, for which this agency is not a substitute. My second objection is quite different. Even if somehow the advocacy agency would change the behavior of the other agencies, it strikes me as wrong in concept and counterproductive as far as the interests of consumers are concerned.

The need for the agency is said to arise from the failure of the other agencies. In virtually every case, the cause of the failure of the other agencies is a cause that would also work upon the agency for consumer advocacy. Lassitude among the employees, over-attention to interest groups, partisanship—all these can certainly affect this agency. It seems to me that we have to ask why this agency should escape the pitfalls of its predecessors. I do not doubt it will do some things differently. When it falls into the pitfalls, it will look different as it falls, but it will be just another manifestation of the same phenomenon of falling.

It bothers me that our basic pro-consumer policy which is embodied in the antitrust laws is not particularly responsive to the political process. If we are to have an intelligent political process, responsibility for framing those laws and for carrying them out ought to be in politically accountable officials, to the extent the matter is not left to private litigation. Those politically accountable officials strike me as being two: Congress and the Antitrust Division of the Department of Justice. To the extent that the courts interpret the antitrust laws in a way that seems inadequate, Congress can amend the laws. To the extent that the Antitrust Division does not carry out antitrust policy, it strikes me that the voters have a remedy. I worry about diffusing responsibility for antitrust enforcement among a number of agencies. At the present time, there are two governmental agencies with authority to present the Supreme Court with an antitrust policy, the Department of Justice and the Federal Trade Commission. If we add this consumer agency, that would be a third governmental agency with its own little antitrust policy up before the Supreme Court. It would not be very long before we had a government with three antitrust policies with everyone passing the buck to everyone else and with very little political accountability on this issue.

The agency for consumer advocacy would necessarily have one practical effect. It would increase the responsibility of the judiciary to make basic regulatory policy. Because it is a governmental agency, its judgment would presumably be entitled to some kind of authoritative weight before the courts. I would like to see some discussion among the proponents of the agency as to why it is they think the courts are capable of making regulatory decisions. I would suggest that one of the principal reasons for establishing the regulatory agencies to begin with was the belief that the courts could not handle and ought not to be asked to handle this kind of decision.

Let me turn to what is, I think, a decisive objection, one which Roger Noll concedes to be the most serious challenge. The very concept of consumer advocacy is defective. Consumers are, in every useful sense, horizontal competitors with diverse tastes and without a single common interest. Gains by one group of consumers are thus very often losses by others. In a world of scarce resources, benefits are rarely gained without cost. Where we want product durability, for example, the trade-off may be between product life and decreased price or between product life and performance and design. Individual consumers will differ on what that trade-off should be. There is no single consumer interest to represent. Confusion exists on this point because of an exceptionally imprecise use of language. One can talk about the maximization of consumer welfare—antitrust lawyers do it all the time—in analyzing economic models. But protecting certain consumers does not maximize consumer welfare any more than protecting competitors maximizes competition. Consumer welfare is not maximized by the government's protecting particular consumers from being outbid by other consumers for scarce resources, just as competition is not enhanced by government's protecting the market share of the least efficient competitor. When the government prohibits a railroad from abandoning an unprofitable line, it is protecting, in every real sense, the consumers of that service. But other consumers who are purchasers of other rail service are paying a subsidy. They are disadvantaged by the government's intervention since they have to pay higher prices on their route to support the unprofitable route.

One agency—two, ten, no matter how many—cannot represent all consumers, and that demonstrably incontestable fact is a fatal blow to the very concept. Legal representation is effective only where there is a single interest to represent. When we do not have a single interest, as with durability or track abandonment, there is a conflict of interest among different consumers and representation is impossible. The representation we will get is not the representation of consumers, but the representation of the judgment of a government

49

bureaucrat. That is why, if we look at the proposals to establish an agency for consumer advocacy, we find they rarely detail with any specificity the grounds on which the agency is to appear before another tribunal to argue for more safety and more durability or against route abandonment. If they did, it would be clear that what was represented was not the interests of consumers at large, but of one group of consumers—perhaps a very small group who appear to have the ear of a bureaucrat.

I fear that the agency will always argue for more quality, no matter what happens to price. It can compel the production of better products, but only by increasing costs. It can compel the dissemination of product information which may be of interest or meaning only to highly educated consumers, also at a cost. These costs must decrease output, particularly the production of cheaper goods. The fear that the proposed agency is likely to have this impact is increased by the fact that the consumerist movement exists. Indeed, Professor Noll seems to assume that the agency for consumer advocacy will look to the consumerist movement for guidance. Now that consumerist movement is largely a middle- or higher-income movement. I really cannot say that we ought to have an agency to represent a particular movement in this society. If we do create the agency, we give this group extra power that other people do not have. It does not seem to me that Professor Noll answers anything by proving that the agency for consumer advocacy would do something different from what other agencies do. That really is not the issue, and what it does might well be worse than what they do.

There is a basic fallacy involved here. Proponents of this agency correctly perceive that the existing scheme endows some groups with monopoly power. In the hope of offsetting it, they propose to increase the monopoly power of another group. The problem with the reasoning here can be set out in this way: if group A (the producers) has monopoly power because of regulation, and groups B, C, D, E, and F (who are consumers) do not, then giving monopoly power to B, the high-income consumers, would as likely disadvantage C, D, E and F as reduce the power of A. When I was doing my apprenticeship at Brookings, I published a book on public employee unions, in which I took the radically unpopular view (radically unpopular then) that there was a chance public employee unions might turn out to be extremely powerful and put our cities in some jeopardy. At that time, the main objection my co-author and I heard everywhere was, "Well, the cities are in the hands of vested interest now. This will decentralize power." But, of course, public employee unionism did not decentralize power; it just empowered another group. I am not saying that the producers will not be hurt by the advocacy agency, but if we want to help all the consumer groups, this agency would be a mistake.

Commentaries

CARL CURTIS: There is one overriding issue that must be considered in determining the future of consumerism. It involves two quite different general courses of action. One course calls for reliance upon individuals, confidence in their intelligence, confidence in open competition and our marketplace economy, and acceptance of responsibility by local authorities with a minimum of regulation by the federal government. This describes the policy to which I adhere. The other course is one of expanding control over all activities by the federal government; it places on the federal government the responsibility of policing the work and business of the country. It causes the federal government to become a guardian for its citizens. It places rules, regulations and controls on the production and distribution of all goods and services; and it leads ultimately to a totally government-controlled economy.

The latter course is based on a lack of confidence in the ability of free men and women to act wisely in their own best interests. It destroys creativeness and innovation; it rejects the belief that the great American system of private enterprise provides more good things at lower costs than any other system in the world. Maximum government involvement in consumer affairs does not work. It is counterproductive because it calls for more government bureaus and employees, more regulations and controls, which mean more delays. It results in tremendous increases in the cost of government—but more than that, it places a burden on the producers of goods that adds materially to their costs and causes consumers to pay more than they would otherwise for everything they need.

I believe that enthusiastic advocates of government-directed consumerism are adding to government regulations, increasing taxes, and increasing the cost of goods and services that our people need to buy. Over-regulation stifles creativity and sacrifices efficiency. Advocates of massive government-directed consumerism do the opposite of what they desire. They render a disservice to consumers.

BENJAMIN ROSENTHAL: There are currently 33 agencies with about 230 bureaus in the federal government that make decisions relating to consumer interests. At the same time, we have agencies that are advocates for other special interests. We have a Department of Labor that generally advocates the cause of labor; we have a Department of Commerce that generally advocates the cause of commercial interests; we have a Department of Agriculture that always advocates the cause of agricultural producers. There is no such spokesman in Washington for the consumer interest.

This consumer agency is not a utopian answer, but in the interest of fairness, it is the best that we can think of at the present. While I believe, with Senator Curtis, that individuals should be able to make judgments, I also believe that the complexities and technological developments in the marketplace preclude many of us from having the information we need to make judgments.

If George Washington took a horse to be shod and the blacksmith did an unsatisfactory job, Washington would have said, "Do it again." Today, when I take my car in to be repaired, I cannot even meet the man who does the repairs. I have no better ability to obtain information on toasters, refrigerators, baby blankets, TVs, than I have to obtain information on cars.

During the course of our industrial development, the federal government established a series of regulatory agencies to protect the consumer and the general public interest—agencies such as the CAB, the Federal Trade Commission, the Federal Power Commission, and the others whose decisions affect the lives—both economically and in safety regulation—of 210 million American consumers. There is no one in Washington who says these agencies have done a good job. Many have done such a poor job that we want to deregulate and eliminate them altogether. Many have, in a sense, become captives of the industries they regulate. The fundamental problem is this: when the telephone company comes in for a rate increase, they show up at the hearing with an adequate battery of lawyers, a platoon of economists, and computerized evidentiary material that was prepared in the shop of the biggest law firm in Washington. They present it adequately, eloquently, elegantly, and their cause is heard. No one presents the case of the consumer in opposition to the rate increase. That cause has never been represented in Washington. In recent years Ralph Nader and occasionally other consumer activists have made a case as best they can. The regulatory agencies do take into account the general public interest, I believe, but how many of us would want our court cases, civil or criminal, to be tried by a prosecutor without a defense attorney, or by a lawyer for the plaintiff without a lawyer for the defendant? The regulatory process really does violence to our Anglo-Saxon system of jurisprudence.

In the House we call the proposal the agency for consumer protection rather than for consumer advocacy, but it is essentially the same agency—one that will gather information and represent the consumer cause. I do not for the life of me understand why anyone would object to that. We envision this agency as having a staff of lawyers about equal to a large law firm in Washington—about 150. We see a budget of $20 to $25 million a year. We see a lean agency that would have the right to appeal to the courts under the administrative rules of the host agency. It would have the same rights as any citizen appearing before any agency.

There is one remaining question: is there an identifiable consumer interest? By using reasonable judgment, reasonable men and women can identify a consumer interest. I think safety in childrens' sleepwear is an identifiable consumer interest. I think a determination of whether a sale of wheat to Russia will increase prices is a matter that could be considered a consumer interest. This agency would bring equity to the marketplace. It would provide a free enterprise system with a degree of competition, and most essentially, it would help provide the factual backup that is necessary for each of us to make an intelligent choice when we go into the complex marketplace.

JOHN ERLENBORN: Catherine May from Washington State, a former colleague in the Congress, once made a fine encapsulated argument against the creation of this agency when she said that the arguments in favor of this agency are based on three premises: first, that the consumer is gullible; second, that the businessman is criminal; and third, that the government is infallible. That sums up some very good arguments against this agency.

One basis for the arguments in favor of this agency involves a kind of elitism. Those who advocate the agency have come to the conclusion that the general public is not smart enough to know what it wants in the marketplace, but that a certain elite group whose members are smarter than the general public can provide this protection in the name of government. There are millions of people in our free enterprise society who are making choices that are valid even though they may be different. Someone may prefer to have a bigger car or a smaller one than I buy, but their choice is as valid as mine. One genius of our system is that out of the hundreds of millions of individual decisions comes a responsive economy to give the people what they want and what they need.

There is no single consumer interest. How should a consumer advocate decide between competing consumer interests? In a power plant siting case, is it in the consumers' interest to have the cheapest power available or is it in the consumers' interest to pay more for power in order to avoid adding heated water to a river? I suggested a few years ago that the consumer advocate faced with this choice should have a public hearing and let the people come in and say what they think the consumer interests are. Mr. Nader's response was, "Oh, no, that would slow down the whole process." But what are we talking about in creating an advocacy agency except slowing down the whole regulatory process?

There is a legitimate consumer concern, and the alternative to the advocacy agency is to encourage the Ralph Naders of this world and the Consumer Federation and others to do the job. I think that as many different consumer interests as are identifiable should be represented before the regulatory agencies. Increasingly in the last few years the agencies have made this possible. They have allowed the public interest law groups, the Consumer Federation, the Sierra Club and other groups to come in on a voluntary basis and to express their arguments and their concerns. With whatever devices may be available (devices such as tax incentives), we should encourage these diverse groups to participate. Unlike any proposed government agency, these voluntary agencies would be supported only to the extent that they were truly representing legitimate consumer concerns. We would then have the best possible consumer representation in this voluntary fashion.

MARK GREEN: I am one of the people who thinks that while consumers have intelligence, they have difficulty smelling carbon monoxide—which is odorless and tasteless—when it seeps into their car and they have difficulty pre-testing drugs that are marketed because they are not scientists. They have difficulty demanding better bumpers from the auto companies because the companies give them no choice. They are not free to eat meat without DES, unless they are told which meat contains DES. They are not free to breathe air that contains no DDT by holding their nostrils every time a DDT particle comes by. It is very difficult for the consumer to recognize technological dangers because they are not as recognizable as in the past. Hence, regulation is required in such situations when the market demonstrably fails to provide essential information.

Ralph Winter reminds me that lawyers are trained to find a problem to every solution. It is his view that this agency will suffer the pitfalls of all the predecessor regulatory agencies. But this agency would advocate; it would not decide. It is not like the ICC that decides at what price a cucumber should go interstate. The consumer advocate would merely present a viewpoint. It would have a very definite and continuous consumer constituency which would interact with it over time. It would have a broad range of interests and lack the specific industry orientation that certain cartel agencies now have. Its budget would be in the range of $15 to $25 million a year. Senator Curtis worried that it might lead to some kind of government takeover, but this agency's budget would amount to about two hours' worth of the Pentagon's budget.

Professor Winter says we need more deregulation, not more regulation. I agree with half of that. I have long urged deregulation of what I call cartel rate-fixing agencies like the ICC which delegates much of its authority to the businesses it is supposed to regulate. But even if Congress should tomorrow pass the bill to deregulate some of these areas, other agencies would continue to exist. As long as health and safety regulation continues to exist, a consumer protection agency is necessary.

Opponents say there is no one consumer interest. The Commerce Department has a $1.7 billion budget of which $61 million this year is to promote business interests. There are small businesses and big businesses; sometimes they compete and have a different approach to issues. There is no one uniform business interest, but the Commerce Department exists. The same is true of small farmers, agri-business and the Agriculture Department. I have not heard critics say that the Agriculture and Commerce Departments should not exist. Professor Winter's argument is that since there is more than one consumer interest, none should be represented by an ACA. I find that unpersuasive. At least an ACA would endorse certain discernible consumer interests and prevent the monopoly of producer argumentation that exists now.

There are certain uniform consumer interests such as opposition to business fraud and crime. We are in the midst of a corporate crime wave as shown by the convictions that have come out of the Special Prosecutor's Office and the SEC along with the admissions about the way business bribes foreign officials for commercial purpose. The ACA could intervene to encourage enforcement of existing laws.

Finally, opponents argue that an ACA would increase costs and harm poor people—that it represents a middle-class movement. An ACA could intervene to provide pressure for lower fuel prices, lower electric utility rates, less contaminated food, and safer drugs. Poor people eat, they take drugs, they have electric bills. I do not see how they would be disadvantaged by many of the positions that an ACA would take. The ACA would promote procedural due process by making a viewpoint known that has historically been ignored. This might increase time and costs, but if we had justice dispensed by inquisitorial judges or had only prosecutors making arguments, justice could be dispensed more quickly but much less fairly than it is now.

PROFESSOR WINTER: Both Representative Rosenthal and Mark Green have analogized the agency for consumer advocacy to the defense counsel in a criminal case. They have raised the question, "Do I think it would be procedurally fair if a defendant in a criminal case were not represented by an attorney?"

I think such lack of representation would not be fair. My position can be illustrated as follows: Suppose we had ten defendants in a criminal case with each one pointing at another saying, "He did it, I didn't." I think it would be more unfair to have one attorney representing all ten than it would be to let each of them represent himself.

Discussion

EDMUND KITCH, University of Chicago: If we look at the Constitution, we will note that an agency was created in that document to be an office of citizen advocacy, not an office of consumer advocacy. This agency was designed to make it possible for the citizens to have effective control over their government. The members of the agency were made subject to reelection at fairly short intervals; citizens were given access to the officials through very simple, direct procedures. This agency, of course, is the Congress. Now I sense that the regulatory agencies, these creatures of Congress, have been carrying on a lot of activities that are in fact quite detrimental to the vast majority of the constituents of Congress. The Congress has the power to revise any decision that those agencies have made. It has the power to change the structure of those agencies in any way it sees fit. Nevertheless, Congress does not seem to have the institutional competence to deal with the problem. Is it really necessary to create another agency that supposedly will be more competent than the Congress?

CONGRESSMAN ROSENTHAL: Congress really has not done a good job of oversight. We have been incompetent in this area because we have generally been unable to contest the bureaucracy. We have not computerized our operations and we have not hired enough staff. Congress is a builder. Most members of Congress like to develop new legislation, but we do not like to do oversight work. The problem is that there is a structural vacuum that should be filled by the creation of this agency that would at a very modest cost correct a deficiency we now perceive has harmed the public interest.

MR. KITCH: Congress stared the President down eyeball-to-eyeball, and I think the country is pleased with the job it did. Perhaps the time has come when Congress can take on an even tougher target, the bureaucracies, and start to deal with them on behalf of the people. This consumer agency may be a proposal for evading any real responsibility on the part of the Congress for dealing with the bureaucracy.

CONGRESSMAN ROSENTHAL: It is not intended to do that. I plead guilty, both individually and collectively for Congress, by saying that we have not done a good job of oversight. Even if we could do a very satisfactory job of oversight, this agency would still be necessary because there is a mechanical defect in the system and this agency can correct it at very modest cost.

CONGRESSMAN ERLENBORN: I will plead guilty also. I think that Congress is inadequate in oversight. I think the reason is that there is no political sex appeal in oversight.

MR. KITCH: But that means Congress will not watch this agency any more than it watches any other agency.

CONGRESSMAN ERLENBORN: That is right.

GOVERNMENT REGULATION:
WHAT KIND OF REFORM?

In the videotaped Round Table that ended the conference, Mr. Nader and Sena-
tor Humphrey stressed the need for stringent regulation in the health and
safety areas and greater accountability on the part of regulators to both the
Congress and the public. Governor Reagan and Professor Houthakker presented
the view that, while some regulation is needed in the health and safety areas,
many present regulations are excessive, unreasonably costly, and not in the
public interest. (Senator Humphrey was delayed by work in the Senate and
was not present for the first half of this discussion.)

EILEEN SHANAHAN, moderator: President Ford has let it be known that eliminating some aspects of government regulation is and ought to be one of the
major issues on which he will run for election in his own right in 1976. He is
for decreasing and even eliminating much existing regulation, but there are those
who hold a different view. Ralph Nader has taken the position that there are
really two kinds of regulation and that we must distinguish very carefully
between them before deciding what to keep and what not to keep.

RALPH NADER: I think it is useful to frame the discussion on the basis of
this distinction. There is health and safety regulation, which deals with such
matters as drugs or food or automobiles, and there is economic regulation, which
deals with the setting of rates or the operation of certain procedures in a given
industry. Of these the former, health and safety regulation, tends to involve
serious human values, such as life and limb, and is less susceptible to market
support because of the dangers latent in automobiles, nuclear power plants,
or drugs.

The second kind of regulation, economic regulation, has been brought about
by a variety of factors. One of these is economic crisis such as the sharp inflationary spiral which led to the creation of the wage-price agencies a few years
ago. Another is a less-than-competitive structure in an industry, as for example
in the natural gas industry. And a third—historically the most common cause
of economic regulation, surprising as it may seem—is the desire of the industries themselves. The truck companies and the airlines, for example, crave regulation by government agencies that will fix their prices at higher-than-competi-
tive levels.

I think it is important to look at regulation in terms of the human needs
of society, so that we do not deal in easy slogans and easy scenarios. We
should ask ourselves what human purpose regulation fulfills, whether it is just
or unjust, whether it is adequate or inadequate, and finally whether there might

---

The full text of this discussion has been published in AEI's Round Table series.

be a better way to improve economic performance, either by more competition, more consumer cooperatives, or more public enterprise.

HENDRIK HOUTHAKKER: I think that Mr. Nader has made a very important distinction between the different types of regulation. Certainly, we do not want to treat health and safety on quite the same level as economic efficiency. Indeed, I might add environmental factors to Mr. Nader's list of causes of regulation, for to some extent they also justify a degree of regulation that is not justified strictly on economic grounds.

However, I may make one qualification: regulation is not automatically good merely because it is intended to protect health, safety, or the environment. These considerations are sometimes used to mask much less desirable ends. I would insist on differentiating between intent and effect. Health regulations, for instance, have an economic aspect: we have to consider whether particular health regulations really are worth their cost.

RONALD REAGAN: I believe that government's principal function is to protect us from each other, not from ourselves. We get onto dangerous ground when we allow government to decide what is good for us. In the field of health and in the economic field, government has grown to such an extent that I am afraid it is showing a lack of respect for the average citizen. With government fostering the idea that the citizen cannot even buy a box of Post Toasties for himself without being cheated, one wonders how voters are supposed to be able to pick for government people who are wise enough to make all these decisions for them? When government starts showing a lack of respect for the people, the people soon start showing a lack of respect for government. Let me give an example how complex and how ridiculous the government has become.

Just recently the Department of Health, Education and Welfare came into a hospital in Ohio and said the plastic liners had to be taken out of the waste baskets because if one of them caught fire the noxious fumes would be injurious to the patients. But the plastic liners had been used only because the Occupational Safety and Health Administration had said they were necessary to protect the employees of the hospital from contamination in handling the waste in the waste baskets. The only thing I figure the hospital can do is put a guard on the steps to scout ahead and see which agency is coming to inspect it next.

PROFESSOR HOUTHAKKER: To some extent the public itself draws the line on regulation. Recently, a requirement for seat belts in every car was put through and it turned out to be so unpopular that now some of the belt requirements are no longer mandatory. Some people may have realized that seat belts did improve the safety of cars. Nevertheless, the public evidently felt that the regulation was not worth the trouble it caused.

MR. NADER: Of course, there are a lot of areas of health and safety regulation that are much more serious than the examples you are giving. For example, 15,000 diabetics are dying every year as a result of the adverse effects of drugs taken for their diabetic condition, and the drug companies did not warn them

58

of these adverse effects even though the companies were aware of them. There are flammable fabrics burning people, burning children, to death. There are very hazardous products on the market. It is easy to give absurd examples, but the serious question is whether the people have an opportunity to decide what government is going to do for them or by them or to them? I do not think these regulatory agencies are open enough to the people to allow that kind of participation.

MR. REAGAN: For every case of a drug that slipped by the Food and Drug Administration and has been harmful to some people, there are dozens of cases of the Food and Drug Administration going too far. The Food and Drug Administration in recent years has gone so far that it has cut by more than half the production of new medicines and drugs in America. We no longer lead the world as we did, and we have added hundreds of millions of dollars to the cost of the drugs that the people must buy. A leading drug company a few years ago had to submit only about seventy-odd pages of data to support a license application and now it has to submit 73,000 such pages. And cases can be made for the thousands and thousands of people who have died or suffered in this country because drugs used in other countries, that have been passed there and proven effective in the market, have been denied them. I think that there have died in this country something more than 40,000 tuberculars who conceivably could have been saved by a drug that has been used widely in the last few years throughout Europe.

MR. NADER: I do not think there is any evidence to support that at all. I think that is part of the propaganda that has been put forward about the Food and Drug Administration. As you know, there are too many useless drugs in the marketplace—the National Academy of Sciences documents this—and many of these drugs should be taken off the market. The Senate Small Business Committee study of the assertions Governor Reagan is making shows that they simply are not supported by the evidence. What we do know is that fortunately our Food and Drug Administration stopped the drug Thalidomide, which caused 10,000 deformed births in Western Europe and Japan, from coming into this country.

I think that what we have to ask ourselves in this discussion is to what extent these agencies can reflect the value system of a population by operating openly, accountably, and subject to citizen or consumer participation. Right now it is big business and the lawyers of big business that have access to these agencies and it is difficult for the public to find out what they are paying for or what they are being exposed to as a result of the behavior of these agencies.

PROFESSOR HOUTHAKKER: I think we can agree that to a large extent the agencies frequently have become much too responsive to the industries they are supposed to control. In fact, in many cases it can be shown that the agencies were created because the industries wanted them, as I think has already been pointed out, and increasing the distance between the two is one reform that would bring about some progress. But there is still the wider question of

59

whether we need that much regulation at all. I am thinking particularly of what was earlier called economic regulation as distinct from health and safety.

Opening up these agencies will do some good, but it will still leave us with the problem that expertise in these industries is naturally concentrated in the industries themselves. Anyone who knows a lot about the petroleum industry is likely to be employed in the petroleum industry, and that may bias his judgment no matter how good his intentions are. That is why I think there is—just from the point of view of an operating democracy—a good case for not inserting the government into areas where expertise is concentrated in the hands of people who also have a direct interest in the outcome of government action. Instead, we should leave the government as much as possible out of the economic field.

MR. NADER: If there is a competitive market structure.

PROFESSOR HOUTHAKKER: I agree with that. Competition is something I think the government should develop and foster by all legitimate means. There are some areas where competition cannot be created, and those I would agree need regulation. There are also areas where competition could exist but is being deliberately suppressed.

MS. SHANAHAN: You mentioned that expertise is to be found chiefly within an industry. I think the proponents of a consumer advocacy agency, and we have one of the leaders of those proponents right here, have suggested that one of the purposes of the agency would be to develop just such expertise. Are you skeptical about the possibility of that?

PROFESSOR HOUTHAKKER: I am. I would not say it is impossible, but I think it is difficult and expensive and unlikely. Instead, I would like to see the government withdraw as much as possible from detailed regulation and not go into areas where highly specific expertise is needed.

Now, there are undoubtedly cases where withdrawal is not desirable. It is clearly not possible to leave drug regulation entirely to the industry, even though I think government may be doing too much regulating in that area.

MR. NADER: We need to give the people who represent large groups—whether they be minority groups or the poor or consumers or the small taxpayer—the funds to get their own specialists and their own lawyers to participate in regulatory agencies, whether concerned with crooked advertising or natural gas prices or what have you. That is why I think the consumer advocacy agency is so important. It does not regulate: instead, it fights bureaucracy; it fights inflation; it injects into the process deliberate skilled information representing a variety of interests that are now not represented, and also advocating procedures to make regulation more fair.

MR. REAGAN: The paperwork required by government is staggering. It is estimated that small businessmen in America spend a total of 130 million man-hours a year filling out government-required forms, which adds about $50 billion a year to the cost of doing business. Now, the consumer pays the cost, because it is a business expense. Then we pay about another $20 billion in taxes so that someone in Washington can handle all the paper. In spite of all of the talk in Washington about improving the situation, this year it is estimated that the small businessman will have to do 20 percent more paperwork than last year. I do not think anyone fully recognizes the extent to which small businesses are regulated.

I think regulation has led to an interlocking bureaucracy. The bureaucracy in government is now being matched by a bureaucracy employed by business to do business with the bureaucracy in government. The two bureaucracies are feeding on each other and neither one of them wants the other to go away because in a sense each employs the other.

MR. NADER: If Governor Reagan makes that his campaign theme next year, he will be making a major contribution to the American dialogue—if he speaks out against corporate socialism, government subsidies of big business, corporations so big they cannot be allowed to fail (which means that only small businesses can go bankrupt). A company that is big like Lockheed can go to Washington instead of going out of business. There is a massive outflow of the taxpayers' revenue into the coffers of the giant corporations. It certainly does not make them more efficient—any more than welfare creates an incentive to work.

MR. REAGAN: I think all of us must ask ourselves how much farther we can go down this road. We know that even now the government is taking virtually half of every dollar earned in the United States. And beyond that, there is a hidden tax that we do not even see in the cost of these regulations passed on from business to the customer. I would like to know how much the cost imposed by government for all of this regulation to supposedly protect us contributes to inflation.

We are the most regulated society this nation has ever seen, and we are paying for it not only in coin of the realm, but also in a greater loss of freedom than any of us realize. We have moved a great distance from the system that originated in this country, a system that was based on the ultimate in individual freedom consistent with an orderly society.

MR. NADER: Of course, I hope we can all agree that a lot of this government regulation is corporate regulation one step removed. I am sure the millions of Americans who are paying skyrocketing electric bills and gas and gasoline bills and telephone bills are not enthralled by the state utility commissions that supposedly regulate the utilities in the public interest.

I think the problem in this country is that the trade associations are over-organized, the corporations are overorganized, the labor unions are well organized, but the consumer and the small taxpayer are not organized. I think it is the function of advocates—critics, politicians, whatever their public role may be—to do everything they can to strengthen those two constituencies—the consumer and the small taxpayer—into organized economic and political forces. They represent the broadest spectrum of interest in our society.

PROFESSOR HOUTHAKKER: Large corporations are not blameless, not by any means, and I am in favor of doing various things about them. But there is a danger of seeing this too much in terms of a class struggle between the poor consumer, the poor small businessman, the poor farmer, on the one hand, and the giant corporations that oppress them, on the other. I think our reality is much more complicated than that. We have to make it clear that the consumer is the ultimate beneficiary of our economic system. If we run it well, he benefits. If we run it poorly, he is the one who pays. That notion, I think, is not generally accepted. There is the opposite tendency to think of the economy in more or less sociological terms, and that is one reason why deregulation has been such an uphill fight.

HUBERT H. HUMPHREY: We should have every committee in Congress exercise legislative oversight—which Congress has not been doing. Congress legislates, turns its programs over to the executive branch, and says, "Go to it." And they go to it—there is no doubt about that: sometimes they go to it with a vengeance. But the Congress does not review the rules and regulations made by the executive branch to implement the basic law the Congress passed. Every committee of Congress ought to exercise legislative oversight on every bill of any consequence, particularly those of economic or social impact. There ought to be periodic reviews of the rules and regulations from each department. Moreover, I think we need to have an economic impact study or evaluation made of every rule and regulation and every piece of legislation that we pass.

And may I suggest that there is no substitute for common sense. Not long ago I was in Morris, Minnesota. We were taking the mentally retarded out of institutions where they are treated more like cattle than like people and putting them into group homes. We have a man and wife who care for six or seven of these retarded people like a family. Now, HEW has rules that require so many square feet per person in this sort of home. It happens this particular home was short one square foot. So HEW sent one person back to an institution and it destroyed him. That person had been coming out of his shell, out of the misery of the big institution, and had been blossoming. Not only that, but it turned out that HEW had not considered the closet space in his room, and there was actually enough space. All that particular situation should have taken was someone with enough brains to say, "This is a minor violation. These people look happy. They are well fed. They are well cared for." Or someone with brains enough to measure a closet. But what it turned out to need was the personal congressional oversight of the junior senator from Minnesota.

MR. NADER: Congressional oversight needs to de developed in two important directions. First, agencies should be expected to report on how their laws are being enforced or violated. You really learn a lot about an agency's impact, in all areas, from compliance reports. The second function of the Congress should be to establish a Civil Service accountability law, so that if citizens around the country are abused by a civil servant, they can challenge and petition for the person to be disciplined or for a review of the government decision. Right now, the only ones who really can do that are those who are very well heeled, with very powerful lawyers in Washington—

MR. REAGAN: But the answer is really that we have tried to centralize too much government at the national level; that we cannot successfully make a myriad of rules that will fit every corner of this country, across the 3,000 miles; that we need more government control and management, particularly of these human problems, back at the local level.

SENATOR HUMPHREY: All I ask is that local government be willing to pay the freight to get competence. I have been a mayor of a city and I have spent a good deal of time working with state and local government officials and legislators. Regrettably, in many of the cities and counties—and particularly at the county level in rural areas—the health departments are not adequate, and the engineering departments are not adequate. Now, with revenue sharing and so on, maybe we can help them firm up. I do agree that if we are going to have flexibility, we must have the people living close to the problem enforcing the rules, and more and more authority has to be vested at the local level.

MR. REAGAN: The federal government has usurped the revenue that ought to remain where it was raised, at the state and local level. Revenue sharing would not be necessary if we left the revenue at the local level and restricted the federal government to those tasks which properly belong to it—the area of national defense and so forth. Let the federal government set the minimum standards which must be met. To me revenue sharing means that the money is collected and passes through those puzzle palaces on the Potomac, and then it comes back to us minus a carrying charge.

SENATOR HUMPHREY: But at least we get the money. Let me say, Governor, in my state, for example, we have a state income tax. We have a good one. But I know two or three states right up here along the eastern seaboard that do not. We have not usurped their revenue. They can institute a state income tax. The money is there. The only reason the federal government uses this taxing power is that it alone is able to tax a large interstate corporation, or other similar sources of revenue.

MR. REAGAN: But when we tax business to remove some of the burden from the little man, the little man winds up paying, because a business tax has to be incorporated in the price of the product. Ultimately only people pay taxes: corporations pass theirs on.

SENATOR HUMPHREY: Only people pay taxes, but there is some equity and some equality of performance when taxes are paid. In my opinion, many of the services that are provided out of tax funds—good roads, good schools, good public health offices, good parks and recreational facilities—are fringe benefits a citizen would never get otherwise, unless he were well-to-do.

Let me say a word about CAB. I come from a state that has little towns. We know that in order to have industry in our little towns—take a town like Worthington, Minnesota—we have to wage big battles with the CAB. If we left the matter to the marketplace, the airlines would have bypassed Worthington. As a matter of fact, the railroads would bypass practically every little farm town we have. They want to run between the big terminals. And the trucks would bypass them all, too.

Now, if the smaller towns—towns of 1,000 or 2,000 people or even 600 or 700 people—should not have a truck or a railroad, if a town of 5,000 should not have an airline coming into it, then we can abolish the CAB and all the regulations in transportation. One has to balance the advantages and disadvantages of CAB regulation because, of course, those major airlines really do not make any money by going into small towns. To go to the small towns is to provide a service, like rural free mail delivery.

MR. REAGAN: If the CAB were done away with and smaller towns lost some of their mainline service, the marketplace would find that there was business for a certain type of airline to go into those communities and would provide it.

SENATOR HUMPHREY: We talk about everyone having to pay his own way. We all pay for each other. Do we want a country or don't we? How would we like to be living out in Nevada, for example, if we could not have a federal highway system going through there? How are we going to develop the remote parts of the country? The postal system, the highway system, the transportation system, the rural electric system, the irrigation systems—look, they tax us in Minnesota for irrigation projects out in the West. Why, that beautiful valley out there in California gets a lot of water—ask the folks in Arizona who think it gets too much.

RITA RICARDO CAMPBELL, Hoover Institution on War, Revolution and Peace: At the beginning of this Round Table, Mr. Nader stated that it could not be proven that people had died because a drug was not approved in the United States, although it had been abroad. Rifampin, which cures tuberculosis, was approved in Italy in 1968, but it was not approved in the United States until many years later. Every year that passed during that period, there were 3,500 to 5,000 deaths in the United States because the drug was not available. I could cite a long list of drugs with similar histories, but rather than do that I suggest that Mr. Nader check the medical literature, specifically the writings of William Wardell, who is both an M.D. and a Ph.D. at the University of Rochester.

My question, addressed to Mr. Nader, is on what basis did he say we could not prove that there was a drug lag when Commissioner Schmidt in recent testimony admitted there had been a drug lag in the United States, although it has now been corrected in many areas?

MR. NADER: A study of the regulation of drugs around the world shows that many countries rely on the Food and Drug Administration's tests and results and findings for their own work. We do the work for a lot of countries abroad. Second, there is a drug lag in another sense, in the removal of worthless or dangerous drugs from the marketplace under the 1962 drug amendments. Panalba, for example, which was killing and injuring thousands of people every year, according to the Academy of Science's report, was on the market for a number of years because of that kind of drug lag. Third, it is very easy to say "x" drug in Italy cures tuberculosis, without also going into its side effects and the availability of other drugs, already approved, that can deal with a similar medical problem.

SENATOR HUMPHREY: Could I just add that the testing procedures are much more strict and prolonged in the United States than they are in other countries. Many of these new drugs are very powerful, and while they do have curative effects, they also have, as Ralph Nader has said, serious side effects. We have known that; and that is why we have had to be very careful.

Cover and book design: Pat Taylor